OFFA'S DYKE

OFFA'S DYKE

DAVID HILL &
MARGARET WORTHINGTON

The
History
Press

First published 2003
This edition forst published 2009

The History Press
The Mill, Brimscombe Port
Stroud, Gloucestershire, GL5 2QG
www.thehistorypress.co.uk

British Library Cataloguing in Publication Data.
A catalogue record for this book is available from the British Library.

ISBN 978 0 7524 1958 9

Typesetting and origination by The History Press
Printed in Great Britain

CONTENTS

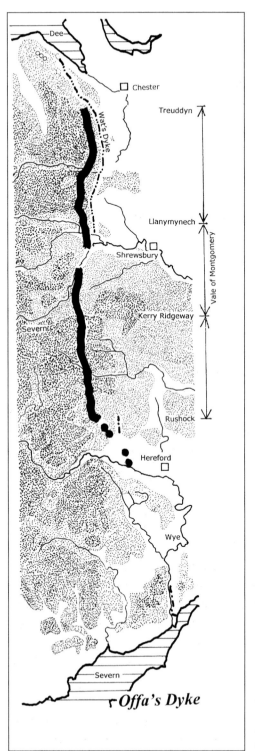

Dee

Chester

Treuddyn

Wat's Dyke

Llanymynech

Shrewsbury

Vale of Montgomery

Kerry Ridgeway

Severn

Rushock

Hereford

Wye

Severn

Offa's Dyke

1 *The solid line marks the limits of Offa's Dyke and the three topographical zones discussed in chapter 3 are marked. Some separate earthworks are also marked*

FOREWORD

A great green bank and ditch strides across the hills and vales of one of the pleasantest parts of these islands, the Welsh Marches. It has been our privilege to spend decades on these earthworks and to work with archaeologists, students, colleagues, and the people who inhabit a string of small towns and villages, particularly the farmers, generous and humorous men and women who have helped us as we struggled to understand the earthwork and the motivation of its builders (**1**).

To spend the day on the shoulder of Rushock Hill, surveying (for much of our work has been survey), photographing, excavating and then to spend the evening in companionship with friends in welcoming cafés, pubs and even barns has been an enriching way of life.

To stand on the crest of Edenhope Hill where the tremendous bank and ditch of Offa's Dyke climb up from the valley of the River Unk, one cannot remain unmoved by the landscape – mainly rough pasture, woods and the mass of Clun Forest off to the west. There are many sections in the 64 miles of the dyke that have this appeal. A few sheep stand in the fields and the occasional long-distance walker passes by (**2**).

However, although one may stand there for hours, little inspiration comes to the enquiring mind. The bank and the ditch remain uncommunicative; in Frank Noble's words, 'it remains a dead monument in an empty landscape'. The purpose of the dyke and an understanding of the people who built it seem almost completely lost to us. It is only by hard work over many years that we have reached any insight and even now our understanding remains limited. This slim volume is an attempt to present our research, to explain our understanding and to clothe the earthwork with some ghosts of the past peoples who struggled on these borders.

To thank individuals after 31 years of effort is impossible. However, two groups in particular have formed the basis of all that we have done:

2 *A familiar sight for walkers as one hill is crested and the next appears beyond the valley. Looking south, the bank is on the left (Mercia) and the ditch on the right (Powys).* Mark Richards, with permission

firstly the farmers and landowners who have watched our comings and goings with a quizzical air but without whose help and permission to work on their land we could not have proceeded. Secondly the students, mainly but not exclusively mature people, who have toiled long and hard in muddy holes in winter and in rock hard trenches in summer. Looking back, we see an idyllic sunlit countryside – but it was not always so.

David Hill and Margaret Worthington
Porth y waen 2003

I

BACKGROUND TO OFFA'S REIGN

This book is intended to be readable as well as informative but in writing it we were faced with a range of audiences, some will reach this through an interest in Offa's Dyke, some through school or university. Others will know a great deal about Anglo-Saxon England and may be discouraged from reading further by this introductory chapter; if so, we advise them to skim straight through to the main body of the book, from chapter 2 onwards.

Offa's Dyke does not explain itself to you. Whilst it is a superb walk, one learns surprisingly little from traversing its length. In fact, it is noticeable that the many visitors who are walking the long-distance footpath quickly accept the Dyke and become fixated on the number of miles they have covered (3). The Dyke has not inspired a Rudyard Kipling, who wrote of the garrison on Hadrian's Wall, nor do we have a mental image of the Saxons to put beside the Hollywood image of Rome, nor an understanding of the people of the kingdom of the Mercians over whom Offa ruled.

No one who has walked any part of the great earthwork that bears Offa's name can fail to be drawn into speculating about him and so, before we attempt to make sense of the largest archaeological monument in Britain, we have to make some sense of Offa and his world. Of Offa himself we have no reliable portrait, the coin images are stylistic conventions (4). We might imagine Offa as grim; no man who overthrew his predecessor and reigned over a kingdom that he successfully expanded during 40 years in a harsh age, did so by a love of poetry and the visual arts. So our image perhaps should be of one of Tolkien's hero kings.

3 *Offa's Dyke on Edenhope Hill (SO 263 883) looking south. The figure walking gives a sense of the massive scale in this upland length*

Offa was king of the Mercians and Emperor of southern Britain. He ruled most of Anglo-Saxon England from AD 757 to 796 and his charters (formal land documents) employed the regnal style 'king of all the English'. He married Cynethryth, whose reputation became tainted by some medieval chroniclers blaming her for the murder of Æthelbert, king of East Anglia. However, unusually for the early medieval period, coins were struck in her name and with a portrait, although like Offa's it is no doubt stylised (**5**). Their children were a son, Egfrith, and four daughters, Eadburh, Ælfled, Ælfthryth and Ethelburga. Eadburh married Beorhtric, king of Wessex, in 789, Ælfled married Ethelred, king of Northumbria on 29 September 792 and Ælfthryth and Ethelburga both became abbesses. Offa had their son, Egfrith, crowned in 787, during Offa's own reign, almost certainly in an attempt to secure the succession, but Egfrith's death soon after his father's meant that he only held the throne for 141 days.

Offa's own claim to the throne of Mercia was obscure. He was the son of Thincfrith, the great-grandson of Eowa who was Penda of Mercia's brother and it was through Eowa that Offa could claim the throne as one of the royal line eligible to be king. He was born an *Ætheling*, a word meaning 'one of the noble, royal, family' and traced

4 The obverse of a Roman coin (above left) shows the probable origin of the stylised head seen on three of Offa's coins, although it is unlikely to be a portrait

5 The name of Offa's wife, Cynethryth, can be seen on the reverse of the coin, starting at the cross at the top and working clockwise. The head on the obverse is said to be female although its similarity to those of Offa (see 4) suggests it is unlikely to be a portrait. Cynethryth is the only queen consort in the period to have coins struck in her own name

his blood back through mythical times to Woden, and the Germanic homelands. Theoretically any *Ætheling* was 'throne-worthy' and had a claim to the succession on the death of a king. Mercia was, and had to be, a warlike state as its borders were all with potentially hostile states (**6**). To the north, across the Humber and the Mersey, Mercia's great Anglian rival, Northumbria, still basked in the afterglow of its 'Golden Age'. South of the Humber and to the east, between Mercia and the sea, lay Lindsey, now part of Lincolnshire. Further to the south-east there was the fiercely independent kingdom of the East Angles, present day Norfolk and Suffolk.

The Mercian border to the south was with the kingdom of the East Saxons, an area rather larger than present-day Essex. To the south-west of

6 *Map of the major kingdoms of Wales and England at the time of Offa*

the East Saxons was the weak kingdom of the Middle Saxons, Middlesex, already having been overrun by both the East Saxons and then by Æthelbald, Offa's predecessor. The prize was London, a town described by the Venerable Bede in around 730 as '. . . a trading centre for many nations who visit it by land and sea'. Across the Thames was Kent, unwilling to accept Mercian hegemony and the most cultured and economically advanced part of Anglo-Saxon England as continental influences and trade came into the island through its ports. There are then, as we progress clockwise, Surrey and the kingdom of the South Saxons, Sussex. Finally, we arrive at the kingdom of the West Saxons, Wessex, which in the century following Offa would become the core of resistance to the Vikings and the heart of a united England, but in Offa's day it was his client kingdom. To the west lay the kingdoms of the Welsh (**7**).

The extent of the kingdom of the Mercians

The name Mercia means 'the people of the *merc*' – that is the people of the boundary. The name survives in The Marches or the Welsh Marches, an area that is now a mixture of Welsh and English. The Mercians seem to have their origins in an Anglian group who settled in the area of the upper Thames and Trent valleys. When the Anglo-Saxons first settled in Britain they were mostly known by their group names rather than a specific area in which they settled. This certainly seems to be true for the Mercians who migrated northwards and westwards. There were of course British people in

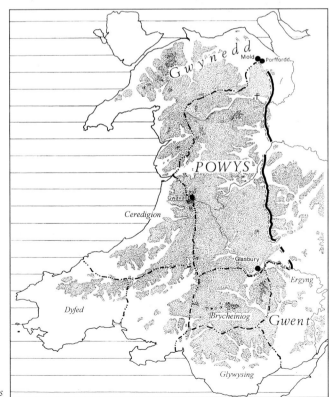

7 *Map of the kingdoms of Wales. Porffordd, Gwavan and Glasbury are places traditionally associated with the boundaries of Powys*

these areas already and some of these and some smaller Anglo-Saxon groups were probably absorbed by the Mercians as they extended their control over a wider area. We know that between AD 600 and 675 the Northumbrian kings under Edwin, Oswald and Oswiu were recognised as *bretwaldas*, an Anglo-Saxon word that seems to mean that they were over-kings of other areas as well as their own. By the end of this period, however, the Northumbrian kings were not as powerful and were becoming isolated from the southern kingdoms. Now it was Mercia that produced strong kings who were able to bring their influence to bear. Kings like Wulfhere, who almost brought Northumbria under his control at the end of the seventh century. He was followed by weak kings until Æthelbald came to the throne in Mercia and eventually regained over-lordship of some areas, but could not bring Northumbria within his power. A charter of AD 736 described him as *Rex Britanniae*, which is possibly a Latin translation of *Bretwalda*. Æthelbald's over-lordship was maintained for about 30 years.

Offa's early years were spent under the rule of an ageing Æthelbald who had latterly become an unpredictable and violent king. He had been a successful king by the standards of the times, but he appears to have become a threat to those around him and as a result in AD 757 he was finally murdered at Seckington, near Tamworth, by his own bodyguard; a most unusual event for a society that laid great store on personal loyalty. There followed civil war in Mercia for a short time as the æthelings, Beornred and Offa, fought for the kingdom. During this time the over-lordship achieved by Æthelbald fell apart. Offa eventually became king of Mercia in AD 757, but it took another seven years before he could re-establish the over-lordship and even then there were some setbacks if we interpret the charter evidence correctly.

Life in Offa's time

The England Offa ruled was our England, the Wales he fought was our Wales, though in Offa's time both of the modern countries were split into a number of separate kingdoms. Rivers, plains, vales, hills and mountains stand unchanged; we live within the same shores but all else has changed. The backbone of Anglo-Saxon England was a rustic community of farmers whose main preoccupations were the growing of bread wheat, the making of cheese, the raising of mutton and beef to go with the bread and the brewing of ale from their own barley. They were mainly self-sufficient, shearing the sheep to provide the wool to be spun and woven into cloth for their clothing and curing the hides of the cattle to provide leather. Their villages covered the land, interspersed with great woods that were managed to provide timber, as most structures were wooden. A nimble, clever, quick-witted and humorous folk to judge by the artefacts and riddles they have left us.

So what was life like for the builders of the Dyke? How did they live? Of course gaining an understanding of the social and agricultural history of the Anglo-Saxons is a life's work and only the briefest outline can be given here. A way into this life is possibly through a set of calendar drawings in the British Library and it might be worthwhile to pause for a moment to consider the history of this manuscript. The book was from a monastic library that was rescued by the Elizabethan collector, Sir Robert Cotton, and he placed it in a bookcase surmounted by a plaster bust of Julius Caesar. Unfortunately, that was not the end of its tribulations as it was in the 'Great Cottonian Fire' of 1731 when many of the manuscripts collected by Robert Cotton were destroyed or damaged. It finally reached a National Collection and is now in the British Library in London where it is known as Cotton (Robert) Julius (Caesar's bust) A (its shelf number) vi (number on the shelf), reflecting its former position in the Cotton Library. The illustrations are small, in a very fine pen and coloured; each page has been remounted and has shrivelled as a result of the fire, the pages are dirty and/or smoke stained, rubbed from handling, scarred where gold leaf has been scraped off, with occasional holes and even blots. In reproductions, there are often parts of the text on the reverse of the parchment showing through. In view of these difficulties, it seemed best to redraw the illustrations using a strong hand lens on the original in an attempt to achieve greater clarity, although it must be realised that there is a loss of artistry in this process.

Once thought to be mere copies of southern European calendars, these illustrations differ in significant details and without a doubt are

8 *A redrawing of the illustrations from an Anglo-Saxon calendar, the British Library manuscript known as Cotton Julius A.vi. From top to bottom the months of January, February, March and April are represented*

true reflections of Anglo-Saxon England. The agricultural landscape we see today in England with fields, farmstead, village and church does not differ greatly to that known in Offa's time.

January: Ploughing (8)

The illustration shows a barefoot boy with a short cloak and an ox-goad who is leading two pairs of oxen that are pulling a wheeled plough. The bearded ploughman is wearing a tunic, leggings and shoes and another man follows him scattering seed, with what may be a sack on his shoulder. The plough was a large and heavy construction of which only two parts were of iron, the coulter or knife that cut the sod and the tip of the ploughshare that cut the furrow. This type of ploughing produces broad ridges and hollows across the fields and traces of this 'ridge and furrow' can still be seen in some fields today, although these date from a more recent time than Offa's. The fields that served the villages were large open fields where wheat and barley were grown. The barley was an important crop that was used to make beer (the Saxon name for barley means beer-grass). Beer, in a very weak form, was the normal drink for everyone as water could be of uncertain quality for drinking. The fields were worked in rotation to rest the soil and were fertilised by the animals who were turned into the fields after the crops had been harvested and also with the muck carried out from the shippens (sheep pens) and byres (for the oxen), together with other material from the settlement that would rot down and had been added to the middens. Nothing was wasted, almost everything was recycled. The major form of traction was the great patient ox, and its use meant that it was fed throughout the winter on stored hay that had been cut from the meadows in July; these fields of permanent grass were often by a stream or river.

February: Pruning vines and land use

Three figures wearing tunics are shown pruning stylised vines with a specialised billhook known as a *win geard seax* in Old English. Vineyards were a common feature in England at this time, when the weather was warmer. The wine was used in the service of the Church but it is likely that the better wines were imported in barrels from southern Europe. Only a small area of the village would have been taken up with vines and other areas would be woods, rough pasture, lanes, houses, a church and churchyard, a mill, streams, plots for beans and peas (good for keeping over winter), flax for the linen cloth, herbs for culinary and medicinal use, plants to use in dying cloth, chicken and duck coops, pasture for the animals, all in addition to the great arable fields.

March: Clearing the land

The men in this illustration are dressed in short tunics, or have tucked them up out of their way. They are preparing a seedbed by digging the ground with a pick or mattock and an asymmetrical wooden spade with a horseshoe-shaped iron tip. The men on the right are planting the seed using a wooden rake very similar to a type of wooden hay rake that can still be bought today.

April: The quality of life

This is a scene of feasting and jollity, and is probably a fanciful one although similar drinking horns and pitchers to those held by the man on the left have been found on a number of excavations. There were occasions for celebration during the year and some surviving manuscripts contain poetry and riddles, some showing a robust humour, that might have been recited at a feast. They tell of songs and feasting, and the Christian calendar had frequent holy days and the agricultural year also had its times for celebration, such as at harvest home, that brought relief from the daily tasks.

May: Shepherd with his sheep (9)

The three most important animals in Anglo-Saxon husbandry were the ox, the sheep and the pig and of these the sheep was the most economically versatile. The animal gave mutton to eat, the majority of milk in the village came from the ewes and some was made into cheese to be stored for the winter. Most of the clothes worn were of woollen cloth made from the wool shorn from their backs. In the summer the sheep would graze the poorer pasture, often in the uplands or on the downs, but in the winter they would be folded (penned in folds) on the arable fields and so help to manure them. One document tells us that the shepherd was allowed to keep the dung from the penned sheep for twelve nights over Christmas, which gives us an idea of how highly this, almost the only fertiliser, was valued.

9 *The months of May, June, July and August*

June: Woodcutting, the woodland

From the left of the drawing, a high-sided oxcart is loaded with a piece of cut and trimmed timber, and a billhook (Old English *wudu-bil*) lies on the ground. A man with an axe trims another piece of timber while a third man swings an axe at a stylised pollarded tree. A pair of yoked oxen, free from pulling the cart for the moment, look on. The timber was not only almost the only fuel available, either as wood or charcoal, it was also the primary building material, a source of tools, fencing, buckets, bowls and of course the carts and the ploughs. The woodland was carefully managed to provide for all these needs and it also provided grazing for pigs, nuts and some fruit. No settlement could survive without its woodland.

July: Haymaking

All the figures in the drawing are shod and have girded tunics. A man sharpens a scythe with a whetstone and on the ground is a bucket, perhaps of water to moisten the whetstone. The second figure is using a pitchfork; the next three are using scythes whilst the last man, bearded and balding, stands with his scythe and looks on. The scythes have cross bars to help the mowers grip them. Hay was the only practical method of storing feed to over-winter the animals. In particular the oxen needed it to keep their strength for the winter ploughing. The hay was dried and stored in haystacks.

August: The harvest

This was the most important part of the year on which the life of the village depended. The illustration shows a man looking on wearing a cloak and holding a spear. A sequence of various men are then shown cutting the wheat with a sickle, gathering it together and binding it before loading it onto the oxcart, which has more solid sides than that used for the timber in June. The sheaves of wheat would then be made into a corn-rick until winter when it was taken to be threshed (see December). The bread made from the grain was the staple food of the community.

September: Swine in the wood (10)

This scene could be regarded in more than one way – are the huntsmen on the left hunting wild swine or protecting the village pigs? It might

10 *The months of September, October, November and December*

be intended to show both aspects of the usefulness of the woodland. The domesticated pigs were still half-wild, hairy creatures living for part of the year on what they could find in the wood such as acorns and beech mast and what they found in the stubble field after harvest; pigs are very good at rooting out perennial weeds. Pigs have large litters and the meat, whether pork, sausages or smoked or salted bacon, was eaten. The bacon was particularly useful as it would keep through the winter months, helping the village to survive.

October: Hunting

The chase was both important for the variety of food it brought to some parts of the community, but also as a major recreation at all levels. Fowling, as seen here, and the chasing of hares, badgers, bears and stags were all popular and each of these creatures were eaten. In the illustration, ducks or geese on the pond are being hunted with hawks and the great goshawk is shown on the left about to fly and a smaller hawk sits on the wrist of the rider. The goshawk would be flown at the large crane on the right of the pond. This was the only hawk capable of dealing with this prized delicacy. The crane is no longer to be found in England but can be identified in the picture by its distinctive tail. The scene is viewed by the bearded figure on horseback who wears a tunic and a cloak, and his horse has a saddle, saddlecloth and long stirrups.

November: Building the fence

From a store of wood, a man carries rods or planks towards a fire. He is wearing a tunic and shoes, a second man, also wearing a tunic, shoes and gartered hose, uses tongs to hold something in the fire. The fire is probably to scorch the end of the timber in an attempt to slow down the rotting of the ground-fast timbers. The other men seem to be warming themselves.

December: Threshing

The illustration shows threshing in a logical sequence from left to right. Two men are using flails to separate the core of the grain from its husk ready for grinding into flour; a third man is using a winnowing fan to remove the chaff (husks) and an important figure is the bearded and balding man who keeps a tally or account of the full baskets by cutting notches into the tally stick. The grain for milling is then taken away in a large basket carried by two men, each with a rough trimmed branch to support them – obviously a heavy load to bear.

These illustrations clearly show the importance of the rural year and the vast majority of people, perhaps as many as 95 per cent, lived directly or indirectly on the land. It was a Christian land and a few memorials survive; a handful of stone-built churches and stone crosses carved with their distinctive designs should remind us of the depth of Anglo-Saxon culture now all but lost to us (**11**). The festivals of the Church provided colour to the life of the folk but there was also a rich culture of poetry, song and decorative art. We seem to be looking at an integrated and developed society. Compared to most periods of history, this was a healthy and even a happy time, although life expectancy could be short.

In this period there were only a few true towns with walls, a market and a mint. These were mainly the centres of bishoprics, such

11 *Carving dating from the eighth century in the style of the 'Mercian School'. The church at Breedon-on-the-Hill, Leicestershire, (see* **15***) contains this and a number of other Anglo-Saxon sculptures.* Derek Seddon, with permission of the church

12 *Coins of Offa with the Archbishops of Canterbury: left Jænbert (AD 765-92) and right Æthelheard (AD 793-805)*

as Hereford and Worcester. The bishops of Rochester and Canterbury minted their own coins (**12**). We know of a number of settlements within Mercia that were defended; some of them we know mainly from their defences as the Saxon levels of the interior have often been destroyed or are buried deep below more modern development. In Mercia Tamworth, Hereford and Worcester would fall within this category of settlement. These centres were where the higher levels of administration were located and they were markets that gave an outlet for the specialist craftspeople who lived in the town. In Tamworth, Offa's 'capital', a contemporary watermill was excavated. This was a complicated structure that required skilled carpentry and complex machinery combining the skills of the town with the produce of the countryside. From our point of view, however, the millstones that were discovered were the most fascinating for they came from an ancient lava field in the Eifel Mountains in Charlemagne's kingdom. Slabs of the lava had been quarried and transported down to the River Rhine, floated on rafts down to the seaport of Dorestad (in modern Holland) from where they were trans-shipped onto seagoing vessels that carried them to England and, by a mixture of river transport and ox carts, they arrived at this inland site. This was a difficult journey as the heartland of Mercia was landlocked and the seaports were on or beyond the boundaries of the kingdom.

A number of large, undefended seaports, known in Old English as *wics*, facilitated international trade. Southampton, Ipswich, London and York were part of a network of similar sites on the continent in present-day northern France and in Holland (**13**) that were dominated by the great and powerful kingdom of the Franks. The English ports were among those that were actively importing fine pottery, wine, oil and millstones and exporting fine wool, cloth and honey. They were also centres for craftsmen such as jewellers and makers of bone and antler combs. A flood of pilgrims passed through the ports. These devout men and women were mainly walking or riding across the wide plains of France, over the dangerous Alps and down through Italy to Rome, the eternal city, home of the Pope. More importantly to the devout, and the Saxons at this time were very devout, this was the burial place of the two great Apostles, Saint Peter and Saint Paul. It was believed that Saint Peter, buried in the great Church of St Peter in Rome, held the keys to the Eternal Kingdom and even today in popular culture he is seen holding the keys to the Pearly Gates. By visiting Rome a pious Saxon could hope for St Peter's help and intercession in reaching Paradise.

What then was the nature of Offa's kingdom? It was ruled by the king with the advice of elders (*ealdormen* or aldermen) in a meeting of

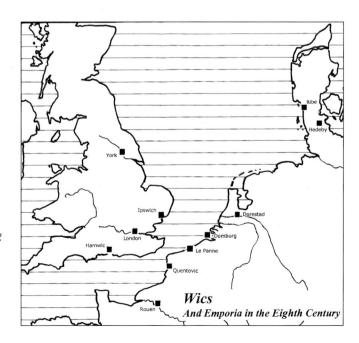

13 *The major trading sites operating during Offa's reign indicating the importance of London for his international trading links*

wise men (the *witan*). These men in turn ruled the various provinces and were themselves advised by local dignitaries, the thanes or *thegns*, who met in the *shiremoots*. And finally we come to the lowest levels of administration, the local moot that would involve representatives of individual villages. Paralleling this civil administration was the hierarchy of the Church. The Pope was the head of the Western Church and a mission from Pope Gregory, led by St Augustine, in AD 597 found a combination of existing Celtic Christianity and pagan Anglo-Saxons. The mission was to convert the pagans to Christianity. By Offa's time, archbishops in Canterbury and in York headed the Anglo-Saxon Church, as today, and the bishops in their centres in provincial towns led the priests. A peripatetic priest would probably have ministered to the villagers from a *minster* church. This supported a group of priests who were responsible for the whole district. Monasteries and nunneries had already been founded and flourished, many under royal patronage.

The monasteries were centres of learning and at the joint Northumbrian monastery of Monkwearmouth and Jarrow the greatest historian of the age, the Venerable Bede, wrote his masterpiece, *A History of the English Church and People*, in Latin. Unfortunately for us his *History* ends in about AD 730, around the time of Offa's birth. The other major source for Anglo-Saxon history, the *Anglo-Saxon Chronicle*, does not begin to be compiled until the century after Offa's death and the entries for Offa's reign are sparse. Contemporary with Offa's reign are a small number of charters, mainly in Latin, legal documents dealing with landholding and privileges that do shed some light on the situation, whereas the few ecclesiastical texts and lives of the saints that survive tell us little of the man or his kingdom.

So here we have an agricultural society where the most substantial men were accustomed to a certain amount of independence and all ranks were capable of defending themselves. Their weaponry was very much related to status, the thegns and the king's companions would own the fabulously expensive swords that were decorated and usually named. This was a dangerous implement only wielded face-to-face by brave men in the front line of battle, even a made-to-order battle-axe was expensive and these swords and battle-axes were treasured heirlooms. As with swords, the type of helmet worn depended on status – they could be complex, reinforced in steel and decorated with plates of bronze. These swords, axes and helmets, together with a battle standard, would mark out the trained and skilful leader. Finally, and again fabulously expensive, was the *byrnie*, the flexible shirt of chain mail often hanging to the knees. All this panoply was necessary for the thegns and the king's companions because they were in the heat of the battle, leading by example and very visible.

Most warriors would have a large round shield made of planks of limewood, chosen because when struck this wood does not splinter easily. The less well-armed men would have a helmet or a stout leather cap with strengthening bands, a padded leather jerkin and a spear. This ash shaft was tipped with a wicked spearhead and the majority of a warband would carry them. Finally the poor, the young or the inexperienced would have little in the way of personal protection and might carry a scythe head on a pole, or a hunting bow from which a shower of arrows could be lethal, or even a mace in the form of a stone lashed to a stick. These less well-armed men and boys lent weight and depth to the battle line, for often they provided a visual impression of force or the weight to push when the battle lines became locked. The well-heeled would often ride to a campaign, but the Anglo-Saxons did not fight as cavalry and would have dismounted at the battlefield to fight on foot.

To this complex world Offa was born of a cadet branch of the royal family of Mercia. We have little to help us to reconstruct the events immediately following Offa's accession but, although the internal disruption after the death of Æthelbald lasted only a short time, it seems to have led to the Mercians losing their grip on the client kingdoms. In particular they lost control of a part of their western border where it ran with the northern Welsh kingdom of Powys. At this time, Powys was ruled by Eliseg who had regained some of the eastern parts of his kingdom that had been taken into Mercia by the expansion of Æthelbald. We therefore have a new king in Mercia, clearly an aggressive and decisive man who had overthrown a weak king and kept the loyalty of his thegns, without whom he would have been unable to rule. He was, however, facing problems on many fronts.

A number of minor kingdoms do seem to have remained under Offa's control from the beginning of his reign. These occupied an area to the south-west of the Mercian heartland. The Hwicce seem to be in the area that became the Worcester diocese, which at this time included Worcestershire (except the extreme north-west), the south-west of Warwickshire and Gloucestershire (except the Forest of Dean) (**14**). It is difficult to interpret the few charters that relate to the Hwicce. Three brothers, Eanberht, Uhtred and Ealdred, seem to have controlled the area and charters by which the ruler of the Hwicce granted land survive from the time of Offa's reign. They describe Uhtred as *regulus*, or ruler, of the Hwicce, but also as *sub-regulus* both titles being used without mention of Offa. However, when Offa grants land to Ealdred he is described as Offa's *sub-regulus* and in another charter Ealdred assigns land with his brother Uhtred's consent and with the consent of Offa, king of Mercia. The exact status of the rulers of the Hwicce is unclear but it does seem that the Hwicce retained some independence during Offa's reign although they also seem to accept some form of over-lordship from Offa.

Further north along the Marches there was the kingdom of the Magonsæte, which probably became a sub-kingdom during Penda's reign and occupied the area of northern Herefordshire and southern Shropshire, an area that could be described as being between the Rivers Severn and Wye, and was to become the Hereford diocese. What is now southern Herefordshire was Welsh Ergyng, a name derived from the Roman name of Arionium, near Ross. To the north we have the Wreocansæte and Tomsæte, included in the Lichfield diocese, which originally included lands as far as Chester (**15**). No charters survive for the Wreocansæte or Tomsæte as separate kingdoms and, although this might be a matter of survival, it could be that Penda had absorbed them more completely into Mercia. Certainly Margaret Gelling, a place-name expert, considers that the place-names of this area are English enough for this to be the case. It seems that these minor kingdoms were an area of stability, even in the early part of Offa's reign.

The reconstruction of the itinerary of the kings of Mercia to AD 871 (**16**) has to be handled with caution, as do all our sources. It is a modern mapping of the places recorded in surviving documents where a king held meetings (*gemot*) of his council (*witan*), places where a king died or was buried and other places mentioned incidentally in a text. Two places really stand out: the royal palace at Tamworth (Staffordshire) in the heart of the kingdom, and London and its

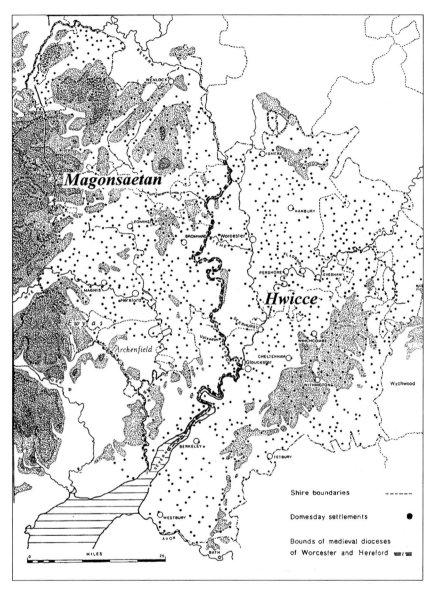

14 *Map showing the areas of the Magonsaetan and the Hwicce*

Magonsaetan

Hwicce

Ewyas

Archenfield

WENLOCK

ISMERE

HANBURY

LEOMINSTER

BROMYARD

Worcester

TEME

FLADBURY

PERSHORE

EVESHAM

AVON

MAGNIS

Hereford

DERHURST

WINCHCOMBE

Upleadon

CHELTENHAM

Gloucester

WITHINGTON

Wychwood

BERKELEY

TETBURY

WESTBURY

AVON

BATH

Shire boundaries

Domesday settlements

Bounds of medieval dioceses
of Worcester and Hereford

0   MILES   25

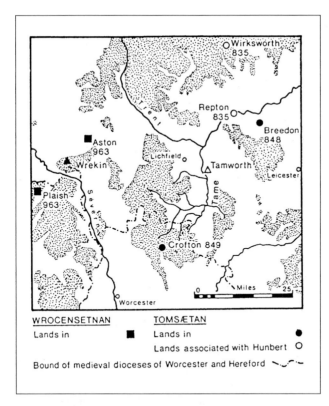

15 *A mapping of places mentioned in contemporary documents in connection with these two peoples, close to the heart of Offa's kingdom, indicates the late survival of knowledge of minor kingdoms incorporated into Mercia*

immediate area including Chelsea, Brentford and Croydon. London was not only an advanced craft and trading centre, a major port (*wic*) but it was also convenient for the clerics and nobility of both Mercia and Kent.

Meetings might be held in a major church or monastery such as Glastonbury, Bath, Canterbury, Lichfield or Repton, or we might assume that other meetings were held in the open air with the participants camping if no major structure was available. Documents would be brought to these meetings, records carried to the site, the king and his court would be accustomed to being peripatetic and the rest of the council were used to travel. Issues of both local and national importance would be discussed and land documents would be signed. It was a time when royal justice could be dispensed but also a real holiday for one and all. No doubt fairs and markets would take place, marriages could be arranged and feasts held. The meetings were often held at the time of religious festivals and so church services would also have played an important part in the proceedings. What these meetings do show clearly is the ease with which the Anglo-Saxons and their court could all travel, and the complexity of state organisation.

The kingdoms that today form Wales were not then a united kingdom but, like England, they were a fractious group of small kingdoms. As far as we can tell, they never united as a single group at this time; indeed the *Anglo-Saxon Chronicle* shows us that they were as likely to ally themselves with an Anglo-Saxon kingdom as with a

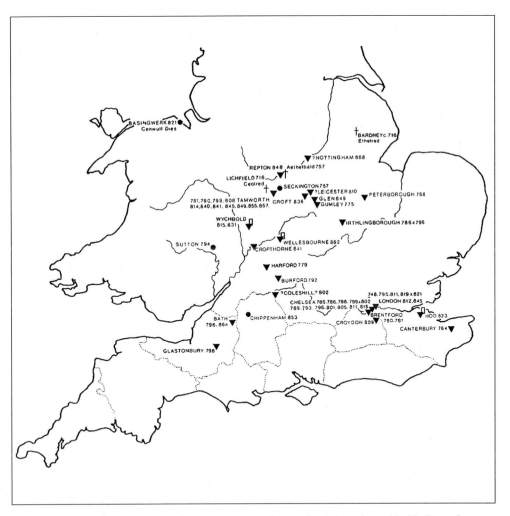

16 *Drawn from contemporary documentary sources, the map shows those places visited by kings of Mercia to AD 871 and indicates the extent of the influence of Mercia*

Welsh one. The popular image of Wales at this time may be of petty kings with their warbands in mountain fastness, but this is far from the truth. Theirs was a society with its own rich culture and language and had been Christian long before the arrival of Anglo-Saxons. The accidents of survival have left us with little evidence but the little we have is important – some writings of saints, bishops and priests, a brief set of annals known as the *Annales Cambriae*, some very early charters for the south-east and some poetry. Archaeologically we have church sites, crosses and inscribed stones in abundance, but the lack of pottery or coins has made occupation sites more difficult to locate. Together the documentary and archaeological evidence give us a shadowy but still vibrant picture of the society. Again, it is one dependent upon agriculture with rich arable valleys and coasts and pastoral uplands producing a way of life that moved from valley to upland with the seasons.

Whatever the early problems, Offa seems to have become a remarkably able king and his laws, though lost to us, are mentioned in Alfred the Great's law code where Alfred says that he collected those laws that he found most just, including those of Offa, king of the Mercians. Offa was also active in church matters and even persuaded the Pope to allow the creation of a third archbishopric at Lichfield, in the heart of the Mercian kingdom. Offa is credited with the institution of 'Peter's Pence', an annual gift from all of the people of his realm to the Pope, a tradition carried on until the time of Henry VIII. The institution of this annual gift may relate to the visit of Pope Hadrian I's Papal Legates in AD 786 as 12 years later a letter from Pope Leo III to King Cenwulf encouraged him to persist with the annual gift to St Peter that Offa had promised in the presence of George and Theophylact – the Legates who came in AD 786.

At this point we must pause to consider the slim body of sources that exists for the early Anglo-Saxon kingdoms and Mercia in particular. It is not easy to assess how cultured or learned the court of King Offa was. There is the chance survival of a letter from Alcuin, the great international churchman, writing to Offa from Charlemagne's Frankish kingdom. The letter appears to indicate that Offa intended his court to be a centre of education and learning, if it was not already one. Otherwise we are dependent on evidence such as the high artistic content of his coins.

Our sources are partial, they are the accidental survivals over the 800 years before texts were collected by scholars in Elizabethan times, and thus the spread of evidence is very random. Archaeologists always have to remind themselves that 'absence of evidence is *not* evidence of absence'; a mistake still sometimes made today. Therefore the map showing where the king was to be found is heavily biased to where charters and other documents survive. Thus some areas, such as the lands of some major churches, are well represented including Canterbury, Winchester, Worcester and Glastonbury, but only Worcester is in the heartland of Offa's kingdom.

Putting this to one side, the burial places of some Mercian kings at Repton makes this a major ecclesiastical centre. It is noteworthy that Offa and his son are not buried there, perhaps showing that they considered it to be the sepulchre of a different and possibly antagonistic branch of the royal family of Mercia. The importance of Tamworth as a 'capital' is emphasised, but otherwise it is clear that kings travelled their realm constantly although the concept of the king 'eating his food rents' is not emphasised by modern scholarship.

Offa was also a player on the wider European stage. His coins speak of trade with Western Europe but an imitation of a gold Arabic dinar by Offa speaks of international trade and a knowledge of the wider world including the east. We also have a small amount of documentary evidence for his relationship with other kings, particularly Charlemagne. Some correspondence between them was preserved in the twelfth-century writings of William of Malmesbury. Here Offa is greeted as a brother by the 'King of the Franks and Lombards and patrician of the Romans' as Charles styles himself. The correspondence speaks of the Church, of pilgrims, their safe conduct through Frankia and their exemption from tolls provided they are not merchants in disguise. The matter of a certain priest from England, who sought Charles' help and whom Charles has sent to Rome to settle a disagreement between the priest and Offa, is also referred to in this letter. They also discuss trade items, black stones that Offa had requested and the size of the cloaks that Offa is exporting to Frankia. Diplomatic gifts are then mentioned, including dalmatics and palls sent to English bishops together with alms to pay for prayers to be said for the soul of Pope Hadrian, and a belt, a Hunnish sword and two silk palls sent to Offa. This is diplomacy at the highest level.

Offa was a national figure, the emperor of southern Britain, the terror of the kings surrounding him. He was also an international figure; after Charlemagne he was the greatest king in western Europe, of an ancient house, important enough to be seen as a threat by the Pope, a correspondent of both Charlemagne (Offa's daughter was sought in marriage by Charlemagne) and the Pope (who despatched legates to agree on the reorganisation of the sees of England). Offa was a possible benefactor of the Holy See, of the *borgo* where the 'Saxon School' was situated in Rome and possibly of the gift of 'Peter's Pence'. His trade network included the striking of a coin in gold imitating those of the Arab trade, of trade arrangements including deals with the Carolingian court over wool and stone. He was also powerful enough to order and see completed the greatest earthwork of its age that is the central theme of this book.

2

EARLY STUDIES OF
OFFA'S DYKE

We begin our discussion not with the earthworks themselves but with an examination of how the knowledge and views of them have changed through the centuries. The only surviving written evidence to have come down to us is much attenuated, a brief mention, almost an aside used to identify Offa. The reference comes in Bishop Asser's *Life of King Alfred* written around AD 893. Although originally from South Wales, Asser spent much of his life at the court of Alfred the Great, to whom he was a close advisor, and the *Life* was written during Alfred's lifetime. Although most writing at Alfred's court was in the vernacular, that is Old English, Asser wrote in Latin, perhaps for the benefit of his colleagues in Wales at St David's or for an educated aristocratic Welsh or Anglo-Saxon audience. He writes:

> *Fuit in Mercia moderno tempore quidam strenuus atque universis circa se regibus et regionibus finitimis formidolosus rex nomine Offa, qui vallum magnum inter Britanniam atque Merciam de mari usque ad mare fieri imperavit . . .*

Stevenson 1904, 12, 14

> There was in Mercia in fairly recent times a certain vigorous king called Offa, who terrified all the neighbouring kings and provinces around him, and who had a great dyke built between Wales and Mercia from sea to sea . . .

Keynes and Lapidge 1983, 71

This single reference during the Anglo-Saxon period has led to much confusion over the exact siting of the Dyke in the nineteenth and twentieth centuries as people, initially including the present authors, have tried to find evidence for a dyke between the Severn Estuary and the Dee Estuary or the Irish Sea coast. Indeed, the debate has continued into the twenty-first century and we hope that the archaeological evidence presented in this volume will help to clarify the situation.

The authenticity of Asser's *Life of King Alfred* was called into question by one scholar in the 1990s when it was suggested that the *Life* was a later work. A number of leading scholars presented good evidence to refute this. One of the present authors (David Hill) pointed out that the geographical distribution of the places discussed in the *Life* was centred on Somerset and Wiltshire, the heart of Alfred's kingdom (**17**). Somerset was also where Asser had been given two monasteries on his arrival at Alfred's court from St David's. On the north Somerset coast they were perhaps intended as resting places between Wessex and South Wales as originally Asser had intended spending six months of the year in each place. In fact, Asser remained with Alfred and later was given the benefice, Exeter.

The suggestion, therefore, that the *Life* was a later work of around the year AD 1000 by a monk at Ramsey, a monastery not mentioned in the text, nor indeed any other East Anglian site, is untenable. It is to be remembered that the premier saint of East Anglia was Edmund, king and martyr, as his life falls within Asser's time it is unlikely that an East Anglian historiographer should omit any mention of his martyrdom. Asser refers only to his death and calls him 'King Edmund', but by the tenth century the chronicler Æthelweard, ealdorman of the western shires, refers to him as Saint Edmund and thus the sanctity is in general usage long before the suggested alternative date for the writing of the *Life of King Alfred*. There are detailed descriptions of Wessex sites in the *Life*, particularly Athelney and Lyng, the latter was out of use by AD 930 and would not have been a noticeable landscape feature by the year 1000. The work of the present author, David Hill, showed that Asser's description of these two sites was accurate. We might further note that several place-names are given in both the Anglo-Saxon form and in the Welsh and that there are occasional quotes from the early 'Old Latin' bible rather than the later 'Vulgate' bible that became current in England during the eighth century. The earlier version had been in general use

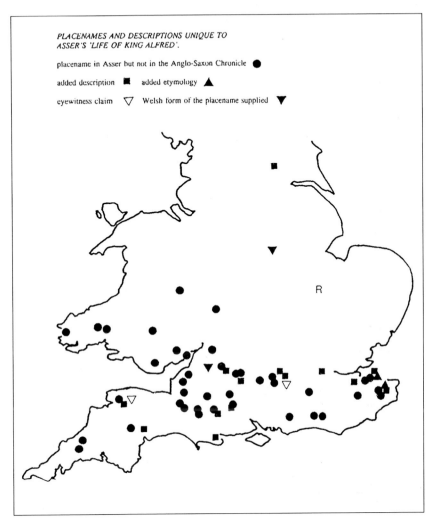

17 *The map indicates the various types of information about place-names and places that are unique to Asser's description and confirms the southern and mainly western focus of his work. The letter R marks the monastery at Ramsey that has recently been claimed by one writer to be the place of composition of the* Life of King Alfred in the Celtic church in the west and Asser, who had been trained at St David's, might well have been familiar with that early version, or extracts from it, even as late as the ninth century.

The authenticity of Asser's *Life of King Alfred* is important to the study of Offa's Dyke as it does represent our only early reference. That this reference was written during Alfred's lifetime, and only 100 years after Offa's reign, means that it is based on the living tradition of people at the court of King Alfred. The reference to the Dyke is not the main point of the tale – it is an aside that simply serves to identify the person who is the main subject of the story, Offa's daughter, Eadburh. Eadburh had married Beorhtric, king of the West Saxons and was seen by them as such an evil woman that they used the title 'king's wife' rather than queen for the next 100 years.

After the early reference in Asser, the sources are blank until a medieval view of the Dyke from which its origins and purpose emerge. The first strand in this model comes from copying and recopying copies of original manuscripts, a process of increasing inaccuracy that also allows the slow accretion of fabulous material to be included. This may sometimes take the form of attempting to explain the form of the visible monument or of popular stories that include the belief that any Welsh person was put to death if found between the two dykes, that is Offa's Dyke and Wat's Dyke to its east. Little in these tales should detain us; they are a source of confusion. The need felt by successive generations to explain the Dykes, linked to the small amount of recorded history, has resulted in the weaving of a popular tradition. This is forever changing and distorting as each generation adds embroideries of its own, but the folklore satisfied people by giving them a framework that explained a major feature in their landscape.

The second strand is the named monument leaving its mark on the place-names. The Dykes have affected the place-names of the localities through which they pass. However, it may be that these secondary names can cause confusion. Throughout England the naming of linear earthworks rarely reflects solid information or purpose and the names of supposed builders include Grim, Woden, the Devil and Robin Hood. Even a stretch of Offa's Dyke was called 'Devil's Dyke' on one eighteenth-century map.

The mapping of Offa's Dyke was, as far as we know, first seen in the work of Speed (1600). Speed was attempting to draw county by county maps that included county boundaries, the most important settlements, rivers and in a cartouche a street map of the county town. These maps were extremely successful and were still being used 200 years after their first publication. When Speed was attempting to draw the map for Flintshire, the local justices would not co-operate in providing the boundaries of the sub-divisions of their county, the hundred boundaries, leaving the map rather devoid of features when compared to other counties. So, for the only county in the series, Speed draws an earthwork that he calls 'Offa's Ditch'. This follows no known line of any earthwork but starts more or less where Offa's Dyke terminates after which it trends across country to end, more or less, where Wat's Dyke ends at Basingwerk. Wat's Dyke is not mentioned on Speed's map. This line marks the confusion between Offa's Dyke and Wat's Dyke, which can be seen on later maps.

In the 1720 map by William Williams titled, *A new map of the counties of Denbigh and Flint*, he shows Offa's Dyke following more or less the Speed line, but seems to realise that Wat's Dyke is a separate entity and so draws it on a line that ends at Flint. In 1778 Thomas Pennant in his book *Tours in Wales* gives an extremely detailed description of the line of Wat's Dyke, justifying this by saying that he has been 'thus minute in giving its course, because it is so often confounded with Offa's ditch'. However, the same confusion is to be seen behind the 1795 John Evans map, though to a lesser extent. This widespread confusion about Wat's Dyke in Flintshire seems to have led to many secondary place-names asserting that this was indeed Offa's Dyke and so we find *Bod Offa*, *Llwyn Offa* and even *Clawdd Offa* on what is indisputably Wat's Dyke.

Another use of place-name evidence is to define the areas where Welsh or English habitation names predominate. This was first noted in Elizabethan times, as in the *Breviarie of Britayne* (*c*.1558), Folio 51, where it is stated: 'And all the townes, and villages almost, whiche be on the East side therof; have their names endinge in there terminations, ton, or ham, wherby it appeareth, that the Saxons, sometime dwelled there. Howbeit now, the Welshmen, in all places, beyond that ditch towards *Lhøegr*: have planted themselves'. Modern scholarship is still teasing out Welsh names that have been Anglicised and English names that have been Welshified along the border.

Before turning to the monuments, therefore, we must look at the documentary sources, for we are today in a period when the available material is, for the most part, recorded, examined and interpreted, but we are a long way from the events. It is important for us to recognise the layers of accretion to the sources together with the disappearances from those sources for they also have something to tell us of the state of the Dykes in the various periods.

The medieval and mythic explanations of Offa's Dyke were finally swept aside by J. Earle in 1857 in his article 'Offa's Dyke in the neighbourhood of Knighton'. His remarks, now 145 years old, are still worth quoting for their sound common sense:

> Everybody who has thoughtfully contemplated these vast undertakings, must have felt a difficulty in determining their use and efficiency. They partake on the one hand of the character of a fence, on the other of a fortification, and yet it is difficult to suppose them to have been either the one or the other. For a mere fence against cattle, or a division of property, the work is too considerable; as a fortification they are far too extensive to allow of the idea that the petty nations they divided were powerful enough to keep them manned. But if we suppose a patrol system, with stations of guard at certain intervals, and the whole under the direction of a chief officer of the king, the living machinery for turning these dykes to practical account is at once supplied. The fenced line then becomes to the nation just what the strand of the sea is – a line too extensive to be kept bristling with spears, but one which needs to be kept jealously watched, lest the invader, or the plunderer, find entry unperceived. We know that our ancestors kept stations of guard on the sea-coast; and we have in the *Beowulf* a lively scene, where a coast-warden espies a ship making for his beat, and rides down to the waterside to meet and challenge the strangers, and demand the meaning of their landing on the territory of his master.
>
> . . . the king of Mercia was wont to keep patrols along the line of Offa's Dyke . . . for the Mercian corps we can speak from evidence. In 855, Burgred, king of Mercia, gave some land to the monastery at *Bloccan leah* (Blockley in Worcestershire) and he freed the said property from certain

wonted burthens. Among other charges to which this land is *not* to be subject, is mentioned 'the feeding and refection of those men whom we call in Saxon, *Walhfæreld*.' Now this word may be rendered, 'the military company on the Welsh service', or 'the *corps d'armée* on the foreign border.' The same body seems to be spoken of in Saxon Chronicle, C., 1053:

Eac Wylsce menn geslogan mycelne dæl Ænglisces folces ðæra weardmanna wið Wæstbyrig

Eke Welsh men slew much deal of English folk of the *wardmen* towards Westbury.

Earle then went on to discuss the 'Ordinance concerning the *Dunsæte*' (appendix 2, source 1) and Gruffydd's raids into Herefordshire in 1052. The 'Ordinance' demonstrates the primacy of cattle tracking in the relations between states on the frontier and speaks of patrols.

We can add to Earle's sound discussion by noting that the *Anglo-Saxon Chronicle* under the year AD 787 not only records the marriage of Beorhtric to Offa's daughter, Eadburh, but also the fact that during Beorhtric's reign three ships of Northmen came and the reeve rode there to escort them to the king's town, one presumes so that they could identify themselves and be given safe conduct. However, these were not traders but raiders and the reeve was killed on the beach. As the *Chronicle* goes on to say, 'these were the first ships of the Danish men which sought out the land of the English race'. Here we have evidence that strange ships arriving on the English coast were met by officials whose job it was to check that everything was in order – a statement of historical record that parallels the fictional scene from *Beowulf* described by Earle.

Furthermore, the *Victoria County History for Shropshire* suggests that the Westbury mentioned in the *Chronicle* entry for AD 1053 is as likely to be Westbury in Shropshire as it is Westbury on Severn in Gloucestershire. The Shropshire Westbury is a short distance to the east of Offa's Dyke and no distance at all for men on horseback. This is discussed further in chapter 5. Unfortunately for scholarship, Earle's work was followed by the maunderings of McKenny Hughes in 1892 who, after some botched excavations on the Dyke near Brymbo (site 70) dallied with the idea that the Dyke was pre-Roman and made by the Ordovices, the Iron Age tribe in North Wales.

The work of the Ordnance Survey throughout the nineteenth century produced maps at various scales that formed the basis of all later work. Their field-by-field examination of the actual remains clarified much, but led to several unrelated portions to both north and south being marked on the maps as 'Offa's Dyke' and these were generally accepted by fieldworkers, including Cyril Fox who based his inventory on the Ordnance Survey information. It is difficult to contemplate the 60-year-long stranglehold that Fox's great inventory had on the thinking about the Dyke, a view that was bolstered by the leading authorities on Anglo-Saxon England, luminaries such as Frank Stenton and Dorothy Whitelock. Earle's words were forgotten.

The 'western frontier works of Mercia' appear in one form or another in every major work on Anglo-Saxon archaeology and society, yet the framework for understanding this group of banks and ditches rests mainly on the fieldwork of Cyril Fox (later Sir Cyril), carried out 70 years ago, and, to a lesser extent, that of Frank Noble. Fox knew of two previous excavations and carried out seven. He spent three weeks each summer from 1925 to 1930 on fieldwork along Offa's Dyke and wrote a report in *Archaeologia Cambrensis* each year. The fieldwork was instigated by Dr (later Sir) Mortimer Wheeler. In 1955 the British Academy published these reports, without alteration, in one volume with a foreword by Sir Frank Merry Stenton and an additional chapter by Fox. Stenton's foreword was a clear statement of the results of Fox's work, provided an historical setting for the Dykes and claimed that, 'the outstanding memorial of its type and period in north-western Europe at last comes fairly into view'. The volume has continued to enjoy a special status ever since.

A guiding principle of Fox was the conviction that most of the earthwork was discernible on the present-day surface and that these surviving remains explained the pattern and purpose of Offa's Dyke. His interpretation of the frontier works is summarised for us in the 1955 volume and outlined here:

> The frontier . . . is held to extend from the sea-coast at or near Prestatyn, Flintshire, to the Severn sea at Sedbury cliff, Gloucestershire . . . The distance measured along the line of the Dyke is 149 miles. The length of constructed earthwork is 81 miles; it is fairly continuous in the centre, intermittent elsewhere. At the northern end lengths amounting to some 16 miles in all, though almost certainly included in the scheme, were never constructed; in the centre the river Severn is the boundary for several miles; at the southern end some 47 miles of the frontier consisted of dense forest and a large river along which an artificial line was necessary in certain places only.

Fox offered a chronological sequence for the Dykes. First came the Short Dykes which were judged to be the earliest of the frontier works and defensive in character, 'the earliest of the "short dykes" then may well be of the age of Penda (632–54)'. Second came Wat's Dyke built by 'Æthelbald (716–57), the principal English ruler of his day', his reign being seen as . . . 'the political and archaeological setting for the construction of Wat's Dyke'.

Finally in Fox's sequence we have Offa's Dyke. The full sequence being outlined in his 1940 lecture to the British Academy and reprinted in 'Offa's Dyke' as follows:

> For a hundred years the Mercians built 'Short Dykes' as and when the circumstances required in the central march, covering such mountain outliers as the Long Mynd and Wenlock Edge. Their Welsh opponents were princes of Powys of Eliseg's dynasty. Towards the close of this phase of activity the idea of a continuous bank-and-ditch frontier was conceived, and put into practice in the geographically well-defined northern sector between the upper Severn with its tributary the Vyrnwy, and the Dee estuary' [i.e. Wat's Dyke]. Half a century, perhaps, thereafter the final effort to define the whole W. frontier of Mercia was undertaken by Offa, bringing into the picture the kingdom of Gwent, in the S. Here . . . much of the left-bank of the Wye and its peninsular tip was given up, or confirmed, to Ffernfail son of Ithel, or one of his sons.

Sir Frank Merry Stenton attempted to define more precisely the context for the building of the Dyke when he stated that:

> So far as can be seen, it was only by slow degrees that Offa rose to the unchallengeable supremacy in the south which permitted the undertaking of a great public work affecting many private interests and demanding sustained control. The *Anglo-Saxon Chronicle* and the charters of the period suggest that Offa's ascendancy cannot have been finally established until 784, at the earliest . . . This tale of harryings is probably complete, and, if so, it allows a peaceful interval of eleven years towards the close of Offa's reign for the building of the Dyke.

This view, of course, accepted the southern portion of the Dyke and influenced the date at which Stenton believed Offa would have been in a position to build a dyke in that area.

Fox saw both the Short Dykes and Wat's Dyke as defensive, the former to protect individual settlements or groups of settlements and the second to defend a kingdom against the Welsh. However, although Fox frequently described Offa's Dyke in military terms, his conclusion was that 'Offa's Dyke marked a boundary, a frontier: it was not a military boundary' but '. . . a boundary defined by treaty or agreement between the men of the hills and the men of the lowlands'.

The twentieth-century view, including that of Fox, had generally been to take Asser's statement that the Dyke ran from 'sea to sea' as a literal fact (discussed in chapter 4) and then to look for a continuous earthwork from the Severn Estuary to the shores of the Dee. Where the earthwork was found to be discontinuous, it became necessary to provide reasons why it had never been built; the two primary explanations offered being that a river provided an adequate alternative, or the forest cover was so dense as to prevent movement through it, an explanation much favoured by Fox.

The line of Offa's Dyke that had been generally accepted in the twentieth century was the result of mapping by the Ordnance Survey and the inventory made by Fox. This line was the starting point for the research by Offa's Dyke Project that is described in this book. It is necessary therefore to examine this generally accepted view of

Offa's Dyke before proceeding to a more detailed examination of the evidence because the excavation and fieldwork undertaken by Offa's Dyke Project has led to a fundamentally different view.

The line identified by Fox is described in general terms below, giving distances for upstanding earthwork and for the gaps in between with distances rounded to the nearest kilometre or quarter mile in most cases. As with all fieldworkers, our starting point was the Ordnance Survey maps and a study of these maps shows that the widely accepted twentieth-century line of Offa's Dyke falls into three broad sections, which are:

a) From the Severn Estuary, along the lower Wye Valley, there is roughly 16km (10 miles) of intermittent earthwork. From the northern end of this earthwork there is a gap of 59.5km (37 miles) to the north of Hereford, perhaps broken by a 0.8km (half mile) fragment of earthwork at English Bicknor (SO 585 170), suggested by Fox to be a part of Offa's Dyke.

Across the Herefordshire Plain, north of the River Wye, there are three fragments of earthwork: in the area of Garnon's Hill (SO 400 445) there is about 2.5km (1.5 miles) of intermittent built earthwork between the River Wye and Yazor; at Lyonshall (SO 328 560) there is a length of clearly defined earthwork for about 2.5km (1.5 miles) and at Bury Hill, Titley on the River Arrow (SO 324 585) there is a further 0.5km (0.3 mile). All three fragments make up only 5.5km (3.3 miles) in the 20km (12.5 miles) of line across the northern plain; that is to say that for three-quarters of the length there is no trace of an earthwork.

Thus in 95km (59.5 miles) of line from the Severn Estuary to the north of the Herefordshire Plain on Rushock Hill (SO 300 595), there are only 22.3km (13.8 miles) of recognised earthwork or less than a quarter of the line.

b) The central section covers a distance of 103km (64 miles), of which 95km (59 miles) is constructed earthwork. There is an almost continuous trace from the north side of the Herefordshire Plain, at Rushock Hill for 54.75km (34 miles) to the River Severn at Buttington (SJ 249 087); then a gap of 8km (5 miles) across the floodplain of the River Severn to Llandrinio (SJ 278 158); followed by 40.25km (25 miles) of almost continuous earthwork from Llandrinio to Treuddyn (SJ 268 577), a distance of 40.25km (25 miles).

c) The northern section covers a length of 35.5km (22 miles) of which 5.75km (3.75 miles) is postulated earthwork, consisting of 3.75km (2.5 miles) of upstanding bank, but also including faint and disputable traces of bank or ditch, and there are 29.75km (18.25 miles) of gaps in between. From Treuddyn there is a gap of 22.75km (14 miles) to the centre of the postulated earthworks at Ysceifiog Circle (SJ 152 753); another gap of 2km (1.25 miles) to a 1.5km (1 mile) length of earthworks centred on Brynbella mound (SJ 130 771); then another gap of 2km (1.25 miles) to a 2.25km (1.5 mile) between Tre-abbot-bach (SJ 106 785) and Trelawnydd (SJ 090 795). From Trelawnydd, there is then a gap of 5.75km (3.5 miles) to the sea at Prestatyn (SJ 060 577), the point that Fox considered to be the northern end of Offa's Dyke.

When Frank Noble came to the Dykes, two decades after Fox had completed his fieldwork, he found that there was no 'school' of studies of the Dyke. Sir Cyril Fox, whilst greatly respected, 'left a dead monument in any empty landscape'. Noble's academic contribution was mainly based on fieldwork, documentary research and contemplation. Influenced by his own understanding of the tenth-century agreement between the West Saxons and a tribe known as the *Dunsæte*, (appendix 2, source 1), hence known as the 'Ordinance concerning the *Dunsæte*', he postulated a 'ridden frontier', with the perceived gaps possibly filled by palisades that had left no surface evidence. His great achievements were to open a debate and, of course, his work on the long-distance footpath.

Finally, we should remember that the monuments themselves still exist and are available as a resource for future study. It should be recognised that there is much to be gained by future workers both from the place-names and, to an even more marked degree, from the structures; for, although the Dykes themselves are being continually abraded and destroyed, they remain an almost unexamined archaeological resource that even our extensive research has not been able to fully explain.

3

THE EVIDENCE

Line and excavations

Before the twentieth century, writers and mapmakers gave the limits of Offa's Dyke as between the River Wye near Hereford and the River Dee and it is a striking fact that it is exactly this middle section that has the most continuous length of upstanding earthwork today. It is only since the nineteenth-century work of the Ordnance Survey that the extended line of earthworks became the 'standard' Offa's Dyke and this was confirmed by Fox. It is therefore proposed in this chapter to look at the central section along the Ordnance Survey line in some detail and draw together our excavations and observations in an attempt to shed some light on the problems of accepting the longer, twentieth-century, length as genuine.

Since the first maps and antiquarian interest in Offa's Dyke, there has been a consensus of opinion that one section, of considerable length, was the earthwork built by King Offa. Any detailed examination, therefore, needs to begin with this part of Offa's Dyke, which has never been seriously questioned; the central length of approximately 103km (64 miles) between Rushock Hill, north of Kington and Treuddyn, near Mold and it is our investigation of this length that is discussed in this chapter (**1**). Once the nature of the monument has been identified between these points, a comparison can be made with other lengths that from time to time have been suggested to be a part of Offa's Dyke, and this is discussed in chapter 6. There is a need to consider the many excavations carried out on these 103km so that information about the various elements of bank, ditch and possible superstructure can be pieced together. The number of sites where it has been possible to examine the bank of

Offa's Dyke has been limited by the fact that such an excavation, if it is to provide answers, needs to be carried out where the bank stands to its greatest height and is least damaged.

Excavation, however, is a destructive process and we would not ourselves wish to destroy the monument we are studying even if it were not protected by law. Thus a number of the excavations listed below were carried out in advance of destruction by modern development, and were not carefully chosen research sites. It will also be clear from this that the search for a palisade has little chance of success when the only opportunities to examine the bank are in areas where the top has long since been eroded away. The results, therefore, are somewhat mixed. The search for the ditch is always more successful and its size makes it unlikely that it can be confused with a field drainage channel. Where an excavation is described that has been carried out by another organisation, it is noted but otherwise all excavations have been completed under the direction of the authors. A complete list of sites in topographical order from south to north is given in appendix 3 and a discussion of our research strategies in appendix 1.

The detailed discussion of the monument takes a view from south to north but the general principles discussed would be equally valid were the description to be from north to south. It should be noted by readers and walkers who follow the detail on a modern 1:25000 Ordnance Survey map that the modern practice of marking national trails, including the Offa's Dyke path, with large, closely spaced green diamonds as well as the traditional broken green line for a footpath, tends to draw the eye to it, and, where the monument and the path are in close relationship, tends to obscure details. Where the path and monument are on slightly different alignments, a false impression of the actual line of the Dyke can easily result. Throughout our research we have consulted the more detailed 1:2500 maps and the nineteenth-century and early twentieth-century 1:25000 maps that gave a clearer picture of where the actual earthwork is situated in the landscape.

Offa's Dyke in the Central Marches is to be seen between Rushock Hill and Treuddyn and throughout there is sufficient surface evidence to present few problems as to where it was built. The bank stands to more than 2.5m (8ft) in many places and the ditch is often visible, still an impressive monument in the landscape despite erosion from

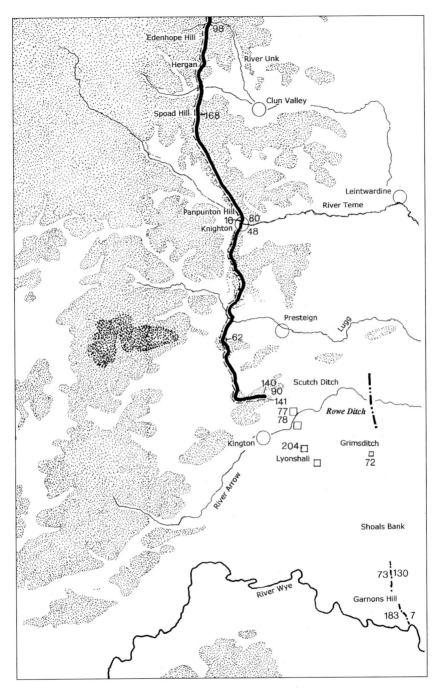

18 *Map of Offa's Dyke from the Herefordshire Plain to the Kerry Ridgeway. The excavated sites are marked and the concentration at the southern end indicates the research into attempting to continue Offa's Dyke across the Herefordshire Plain. The nine sites excavated on the Rowe Ditch have not been indicated but are listed in appendix 2*

the bank and silting of the ditch. The line between Rushock Hill and Treuddyn crosses several topographical zones of the Welsh Marches and there are three main recognisable areas. The first is found travelling north from Rushock Hill to the Kerry Ridgeway where the Dyke follows an almost direct north/south line, but one which, on a closer examination, follows a sinuous course. When walking this section it becomes clear that the line chosen is in fact a direct route across the grain of the country, but that the line is also sensitive to the topography and to the domination of the view to the west.

Rushock Hill to the Kerry Ridgeway (18)

In the south, above the little town of Kington, the first sighting of the Dyke is on Rushock Hill, where the view south is clear across the Herefordshire Plain to the River Wye, above Hereford, and beyond. As seen today, the Dyke begins as a moderately large bank with evidence for the western ditch. The Ordnance Survey maps show an earthwork extending into the woods on a north-east alignment, but our fieldwork and excavation have shown this to be a false line following a field boundary. The search for evidence of Offa's Dyke continuing across the Herefordshire Plain is discussed more fully in chapter 6. From Rushock Hill north, the Dyke curves round the western shoulder of Herrock Hill, from where it begins its trace across countryside of hills and valleys by climbing diagonally to the forward slope of the next small rounded hill and dropping down diagonally to the next valley bottom. Many small rivers and steams flow in this complex topography and it is noticeable that the Dyke holds the watershed on the hills and manages to approach and cross the valleys at a point where only one water crossing has to be made. Thus from Herrock Hill the Hindwell Brook is crossed below its confluence with several small tributaries and a similar pattern is to be seen at the crossing of the River Lugg. As it approaches the River Teme, however, it first crosses a tributary stream before the river itself, but by doing so it avoids a tributary flowing from the north and keeps a shorter, more direct route to Panpunton Hill.

The countryside is now changing and the nature of the course of the Dyke changes with it. Although it continues to be sensitive to rounded hills, these tend to be on long ridges that trend east/west and on these the Dyke takes a more direct line from the top of the slope to the valley bottom and up the other side. First, on Panpunton Hill above Knighton, it climbs steadily whilst curving round the western slope above the valley of the River Teme. A long climb that curves round the head of a small stream as it approaches Cwm-sanahan Hill, but crosses the next tributary near Garbett Hall to avoid a considerable detour round the head of this stream. The line then holds the watershed over Llanfair Hill but crosses a small stream near Springhill Farm to follow what seems, at first sight, an unlikely line on the eastern slope of Spoad Hill as it drops down into the Clun Valley, where views to the west are restricted. However, the earthwork is visible, the line is direct and the reason is clearly to be seen in the valley bottom where the crossing is immediately below the confluence of the Folly Brook with the River Clun. It is interesting to note how these crossing points and the hills above them are often the site of fortifications of both earlier Iron Age hillforts and later Norman motte-and-bailey castles.

Climbing steeply out of the Clun Valley, Offa's Dyke again follows a more sinuous course as it holds the western slope on the hills and, where possible, avoids water crossings. It is on this length that a 'right-angled turn' on Hergan Bank, much discussed by Fox, occurs. In the past this has been suggested to be a place where two teams of workers building the Dyke approached each other from north and from south only to find that they did not line up, which is why the right angle resulted. However, following the pattern observed to the south, it can be seen that before reaching Hergan, the Dyke is holding a contour that curves round a small hill and has to turn, with the contours, quite sharply to gain the lower slopes of Hergan Hill (SO 263 854). The landscape here is very close with many small hills and streams. On the slope of Hergan Hill, the Dyke is above what is today a shallow, dry valley, although rushy growth in the bottom suggests that in wet weather it is boggy (**19**). To the west there is a small, rounded hill that does not allow total command of the area to the west from this point. The structure of the bank and ditch here take the form, usually found when the line runs along the contour of a steep hill, of a steepening of the natural slope, with a slight bank on the upward slope, but also with a ditch and counterscarp bank to the west giving a very strong defence with

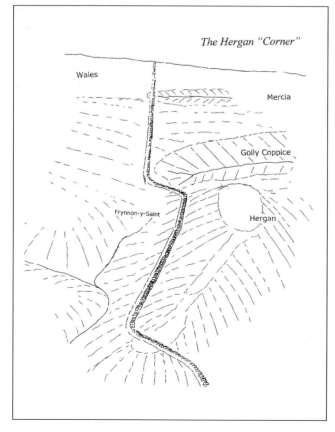

The Hergan "Corner"

Wales

Mercia

Golly Coppice

Frynnon-y-Saint

Hergan

19 *The 'right angle' at Hergan Corner (see* **18***). The photograph and drawing clearly show that the abrupt change in the line at this point is a deliberate decision to avoid the watercourses and not a mistake by the Anglo-Saxon workforce* limited effort. The line of the Dyke then turns back onto a direct north/south line towards Middle Knuck on the skyline. By taking this right-angled line, the surveyor is again avoiding the necessity of crossing watercourses. The direct line over the low hill that blocks the view of the actual line taken would necessitate crossing two streams. By running on round the hill and then turning sharply where it does, it avoids not only these two streams but also two east-flowing streams. The line is in fact very carefully chosen with great regard for the local topography whilst keeping the long-distance objective in view; it is economical of build and minimises both the effects of the dead ground in one section and the number of streams crossed. Thus, the mysterious right angle is explained by the realisation that the builders of the Dyke were extremely sensitive to local topography and kept a balance between the direct line they wished to take between two points and the need to avoid the difficulty of crossing water wherever possible.

From Middle Knuck, the line plunges almost vertically down to Churchtown, again crossing the stream in the valley below a tributary, before climbing directly up to Edenhope Hill only to plunge down again into the valley of the River Unk and up the other side to the Kerry Ridgeway. In this section the Dyke, in some places, is still a magnificent monument dominating the landscape.

Moving from the overview, the next paragraphs consider the same length of Offa's Dyke that has been described above but deal with the detail of the excavations. Eight excavations have been carried out within this section.

Site 62, Newcastle Hill (SO 270 639)
A limited excavation took place at this site to confirm that the gap in the bank and ditch was the result of it being crossed by post-medieval drainage and was not an original gap in the monument (see drawing of gateways, **28**).

Site 48, Frydd Road, Knighton (SO 285 721) CPAT
Excavations were carried out in 1976 in advance of a road-widening scheme. South of this road a bungalow stands on the line of the Dyke and further south the bank has been much damaged and reduced to the size of a hedge bank. To the north, where it was to be cut back,

it survived to a much greater height with evidence for the ditch still visible. On excavation, it became clear that the base of the bank was more than 0.5m below the present ground level and therefore more survived than had originally been thought. The bank was found to be 8m wide and 2m high. The bank was made up of turfs and material dug from the ditch. The various layers within the bank seem to suggest that the material from the ditch was dumped directly onto the bank as the finer upper soils were at the bottom and the coarser soils and stone were at the top. In one area some shallow scoops were noted to the east of the bank that might have provided additional material for its build. Here the bank did not seem to be a careful construction of stacked turfs forming the face and holding back the soil. Instead the turfs had been thrown down on the newly cleared surface, sometimes towards the front of the bank and sometimes towards the rear. Although a sinuous line of turfs was recognised, it was not felt by the excavators to be straight enough to be a marking out bank. No evidence was found for any timber within the body of the bank, nor as a revetment to the front or to the rear. A single slope, at least 10m in length, from the top of the bank to the bottom of the ditch, seems to have been built at this point. The report also noted that here the shaly subsoil that formed the west face of the bank above the ditch would have been very difficult to climb. This excavation, carried out over a two-week period, has provided one of the most complete sections of bank and ditch in this upland area.

Site 16 Pinner's Hole, Knighton (SO 284 726)

A partial examination of the bank of this scheduled section of dyke was made in 1973 when permission was given for an examination of the superficial layers only. Therefore only the turf and topsoil were removed from the bank. These upper layers were removed in an attempt to examine evidence for a wall or a palisade. A partially tumbled wall was indeed found but sealed beneath it were sherds of medieval pottery. There can be no doubt that the bank and ditch in this section are Offa's Dyke and it seems to have been utilised as the base for the medieval town wall that is known to have existed but the course of which is not fully understood. The ditch on the west was excavated. This was an important stage in our understanding of the Dyke, firstly because it showed that the ditch was excavated through difficult geology and was important because, at an excavation at Tre-abbot-bach (site 18) we could not find the ditch and one theory had been that the rock was too hard to dig a ditch. Secondly, it was clear at Pinner's Hole that the balance between cut and fill was uneven; in other words, the amount of material from the ditch was insufficient to make the bank.

Site 80 Llanfair Waterdine, Kinsley Wood (SO 284 735)

The exact line of Offa's Dyke after it crosses from the southern bank of the River Teme in Knighton to the north bank and approaches Panpunton Hill has not been identified. This excavation was to test one of the proposed lines, but the slight bank that was visible was a former hedge on the parish boundary with no evidence for a substantial ditch and therefore was not Offa's Dyke. This excavation was carried out in extremely wet conditions on a steep slope resulting in one of a series of cartoons drawn by Jill Burton, one of our group (**20**).

The considerable distance between the above excavations and those that follow is explained by the good condition of the upstanding Dyke and the lack of any threat to it that would necessitate excavation.

'SOME SITES ARE MORE DIFFICULT THAN OTHERS'

20 *Cartoon of the excavations at site 80, Kinsley Wood. The difficulty of keeping one's footing on the steep slope in the wet conditions made this a memorable site! This is one of a series of cartoons drawn by the late Jill Burton, an Extra-Mural student and good friend*

Site 98 River Unk, Mainstone (SO 263 887)

In 1993 drainage pipes were to be laid through the line of Offa's Dyke on the southern side of the valley of the River Unk. Two machine-cut trenches for the pipe provided a partial section of the bank that did not reach the old ground surface in the southern trench and a ditch section in the northern trench (**21**). The bank consisted of layers of gravel and clay; some layers were stone free and others not. The section did not add to our knowledge as it was entirely consistent with upcast from the ditch and no new evidence for the structure of the bank was observed. The northern trench was situated where the bank had already disappeared and the trench for the pipe was deepened to allow the full ditch section to be recovered. Here the U-shaped ditch was remarkable for its size, being 9m wide and over 3.5m deep, compared to the average dimensions of 7m wide and 2m deep. The bottom of the ditch was deeper than that of the stony bed of the nearby river, which disappears underground in prolonged dry periods. It would appear that such a substantial ditch could only have been hand-excavated during such a dry period. That it was possible to excavate and record this ditch in the April of 1993 was partially due to it being cut mechanically and swiftly. The recording was done from the outside of the somewhat unstable trench. The water was completely below ground in the riverbed in this dry year although in other years at this time the bridge over the River Unk in the nearby lane had been closed as the river flooded.

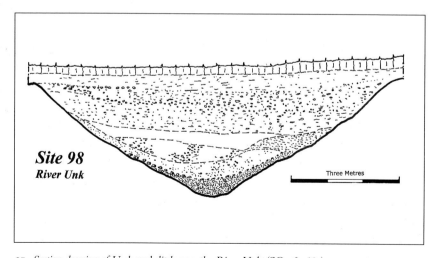

Site 98
River Unk

Three Metres

21 *Section drawing of U-shaped ditch near the River Unk (SO 263 887)*

Site 128 Nutwood, Edenhope (SO 259 893)

In contrast to the excavation by the River Unk (site 98), this excavation was on the hillside on the north side of the Unk Valley. It was clear from field walking that this length of Offa's Dyke was a particularly problematic impediment to the surface drainage. The question of how the builders of the Dyke had solved this problem throughout the whole length of Offa's Dyke had been under consideration as a part of our research and this seemed a suitable place for an investigation.

Two excavations took place here, one where the surface evidence for the bank was slight but excavation across these remains showed that a considerable depth of silt had built up against its upslope, eastern face and that this had masked the bank that still stood a metre high below the modern surface of the field. The second excavation removed the turf and topsoil from a badly eroded area of bank adjacent to a modern cut through the earthwork. This allowed a reasonably large surface of the lower part of the bank to be examined and some evidence for the use of turfs in the build of the bank was observed. The silt and modern cuts through the bank were clear indications of the need for some form of drainage through the bank as part of its original construction, to prevent the area on the Mercian side becoming a quagmire, but no evidence was found for a feature that could be interpreted as a culvert in our excavations. A possible explanation for lack of evidence for drainage through the Dyke, both here and in other excavations, is that brushwood culverts may have been laid at intervals in areas where they were seen to be necessary. Unfortunately the evidence for this type of drain would be extremely hard to find after such a long period of time.

Site 56 Kerry Ridgeway, Castlewright (SO 258 896)

This excavation was following up the suggestion by Fox that this was the site of an original gateway through the Dyke. The rounded spine of this hill carried a prehistoric route known as the Kerry Ridgeway. The point at which the Dyke crossed this Ridgeway would certainly be a potential crossing point between the east and west sides of the Dyke. The specific question of whether the Dyke design included such a crossing point will be discussed later. Suffice it to say that evidence for a full-scale Offan ditch was recovered and this break in the Dyke would seem to be a later field entrance, with no evidence being recovered for it having been the earlier course of the Ridgeway route, and can be contrasted with site 154 adjacent to the Chirbury Road where the cobbled surface of an early road was found (see below).

Site 20, Castlewright, Agger (SO 259 896) Houghton

An earlier investigation on the northern side of the present Ridgeway road had been carried out between 1957 and 1960 by A.W.J. Houghton. Three excavations are recorded running north from the road side and are all situated to the west of Offa's Dyke, which is still to be seen standing to a good height on the northern side of the modern road with a farm track situated in the ditch as it runs northwards. Houghton's investigation was to confirm the presence of a Roman road along the Ridgeway but has implications for the postulated original gateway through the Dyke in this area and is therefore discussed further below.

Vale of Montgomery to the River Vyrnwy (22)

The second zone crossed by Offa's Dyke is the lowlands of the Vale of Montgomery, the Vale of Powys and the valleys of the River Severn and the River Vyrnwy. The monument is again upstanding for much of this length and keeps an almost straight line. From the Kerry Ridgeway the line curves gently down the western slope of a spur of land that gives a less steep approach to the valley bottom than the land to either side. From the Drewin Farm the line is direct along the eastern side of the Vale of Montgomery. Minor deviations from the line occur where the western slope of a slight knoll offers a better view to the west, but the Caebitra stream, the Lack Brook and the major River Camlad are crossed directly as no deviation would offer a better crossing point. The line taken to the north side of the River Camlad trends slightly to the north-west to hold a position that gives the best views to the west. It is worth noticing here that there is a line of later Norman mottes, after the one at Brompton, that hold a line that is east of Offa's Dyke. The vale to the west is fully under the control of the Norman overlords and is dominated first by Hen Domen and then

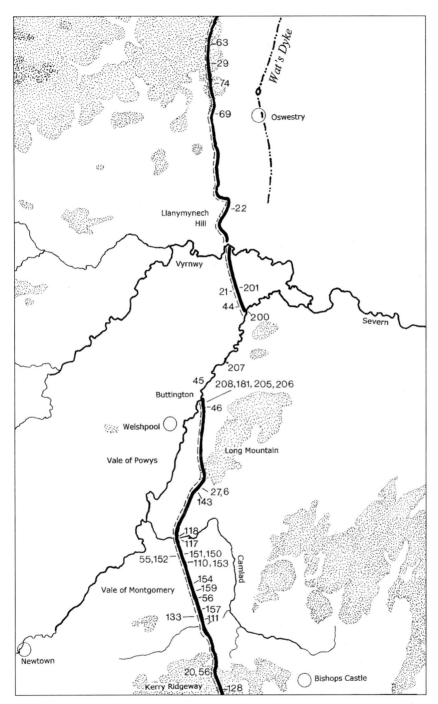

22 *Map of Offa's Dyke from the Kerry Ridgeway to Chirk. The concentration of excavations in the Vale of Montgomery indicate the research into possible original gateways (see* **28***), and that near Buttington indicate the research into the line of Offa's Dyke as it approaches the River Severn*

Montgomery Castle. It would seem that the aim of the eastern line of Norman defences is more concerned with the view to the east than to the west. The suggestion must surely be, therefore, that in Offa's time the land to the east was fully under Mercian control, as the Dyke is sited to hold the view west but not to the east as no threat is perceived from this direction.

There have been 28 excavations in this lowland zone, 14 of which were in the section described above. This has in some respects been our research area for testing various theories and nine of the sites (sites 55 and 150 to 157) were concerned with our detailed investigation into gateways and are therefore discussed under Gateways (p.89). The remaining nine sites are discussed below.

Site 111, The Blue Bell, Brompton and Rhiston (SO 251 933) SCC
In 1984, Shropshire County Council Highways Department were carrying out preliminary work prior to road widening. We had been in contact with the engineer in charge of the work as it was possible that evidence for the ditch of Offa's Dyke could be found within their excavations and he had agreed to telephone when the excavation was fully open. Unfortunately, it was impossible to be present to observe the trench, but the engineer made detailed drawings of the location, shape and depth of the base of the ditch and also took a series of Polaroid photographs. It is absolutely clear from this evidence that the earthwork had been present prior to the present roadway. Although not part of our original research design, this evidence forms part of our investigation into the possibility of original crossing-places through the Dyke in the Vale of Montgomery.

Site 133 Brompton Hall Paddock, Brompton and Rhiston (SO 251 933)
Slight remains of the bank were visible in the field to the north of the road outside the Blue Bell Hotel and were investigated prior to destruction by road widening. Excavation showed that the bank survived to approximately a metre high, mainly below the present ground surface. The western face of the bank was a stiff loam, with turf lines visible forming the front of the bank at a steep angle of 65 degrees with what appeared to be degraded turf forming a more gentle slope of 45 degrees to its rear. The ditch was not excavated at this site, nor was the relationship between bank and ditch investigated,

but the soils to the west appeared to be re-deposited bank material, presumably pushed down in relatively modern times to give a flat field.

Site 110 Barker's Fort, Chirbury (SO 236 974)

A little more than 3km to the north, a site adjacent to the Chirbury Road and to the east of the Dyke had appeared from air photographs to be a large rectilinear enclosure attached to the bank of Offa's Dyke. This was investigated by examining early maps and by geophysical survey. These showed that the two postulated sides to the east and south were associated with the medieval ridge and furrow, whilst the third side, at the north, appeared on an early map as the original line of the road and our investigation of a possible gateway at site 154 (SO 235 972) across a gap that had been suggested to be an original crossing point, produced a substantial cobbled surface confirming that this was indeed the pre-turnpike roadway. The ditch of Offa's Dyke was, however, present below the old road surface and was therefore not an original opening through the earthwork. The fourth side of the apparent rectangular feature was the bank of Offa's Dyke itself, here standing to a considerable height with a deep ditch to its west.

Within the postulated rectilinear enclosure discussed above was a horseshoe-shaped feature with a small mound at its centre. An excavation across the line of this feature found a shallow ditch that was little deeper than the visible surface evidence. This shallow feature appears to lie over the medieval ridge and furrow and is therefore presumed to post-date it. Samples were taken by Tony Clark of English Heritage and the feature was found to be modern. None of these features would appear to have any connection with the form and purpose of Offa's Dyke which here continues as a single line of bank and ditch.

Sites 117 (SO 232 992) and 118 (SO 232 993)

These sites were excavated to the north and south of the River Camlad and the full-scale ditch was found adjacent to the river at both sites. This strongly suggests that Offa's Dyke was built right up to the river-banks, as any significant changes in the course of the river would have destroyed all evidence. This conclusion was strengthened by the obser-vation of distinct differences in the material of the banks exposed after serious winter flooding had recently removed vegetation from the face of the banks. These anomalies on both the southern and northern banks were exactly in line with the known course of the Dyke.

From the Camlad Valley, Offa's Dyke climbs the steep slope to the north and curves round the western slope of the valley side to resume its straight alignment, now with a north-easterly trend. The line is again holding the western slope of an upland area that overlooks the valley of the River Severn. Both the bank and the ditch are clearly visible for most of this length and the line is not in doubt here until the floodplain of the River Severn is reached near Buttington.

Site 6, Bryn Hafod, Forden (SJ 243 028) Fox
Site 27, Bryn Hafod, Forden (SJ 243 028)

Two excavations were carried out on this line, near Court House at Forden. The first was in 1929 by Cyril Fox where the bank was investigated and a bank 12m (36ft) wide at its base was uncovered almost completely buried below the present level of the field. The lip of the ditch was identified, but the ditch was not excavated. The reason for this excavation was not to identify the Dyke where it might appear to be missing but to examine the possibility that it followed the postulated Roman road to the fort at Forden Gaer on the River Severn (SO 207 990). No evidence was found for any metalled road under or adjacent to the bank, nor were any artefacts recovered.

In 1976 this excavation was re-opened by Offa's Dyke Project to locate the layer below the bank that Fox had marked as 'decayed vegetation' on his section drawing. It was hoped that seed remains or pollen might be recovered that would give evidence of the land use prior to the building of the Dyke. This was to test a then still current theory put forward by Fox that where the Dyke followed a more sinuous course it did so to avoid obstacles such as wooded country and that where it was straight it had been built across cleared agricultural land. Here, of course, the Dyke had a straight course that Fox had shown was unlikely to be because of a Roman road. The Fox trench was found to be only 2ft wide and was therefore widened by approximately 2½ft (0.75m) to each side to make it safe and to expose undisturbed samples.

When the Fox drawing was compared with the newly cut section, no evidence for decayed vegetation was found either within a thin layer of clay, thought to represent the ground surface, or elsewhere within the section. However, what was at the time interpreted as a turf marking out bank was found beneath the bank and resting on the thin layer of clay that was thought to represent either an old ground surface or decayed turf. It was noted that there was no evidence of a normal soil profile below this layer and it therefore seems likely that both the turf and the topsoil had been removed. It was further noted that the sequence of material in the body of the bank suggested that the core of the bank, particularly its western side, was made up of the strong yellow clay from the ditch. This was overlaid by a layer that tailed-out to the east by a mixture of subsoil and clay, and above this a more humic brown clay topsoil had been laid. There was evidence within the bank of the remains of turf.

Re-examining these two sections 25 years after the second excavation, it seems that the strong line marked on Fox's drawing at the base of the bank and interrupted by the cut for the ditch is the same as the clay layer found in our excavation and interpreted as the old ground surface. A small arrow descends from this layer on Fox's drawing and points to the words 'decayed vegetation here'. When the position of this arrow is compared to our section, it seems that this could well be the turf we found and interpreted as a marking out bank in our excavation. Thus the two excavations found detailed evidence, but the interpretation differs as we have the advantage of comparing it with a larger number of excavations.

The straight line of Offa's Dyke is continued to the foot of the Long Mountain where the valley of the River Severn to the west narrows slightly. The Dyke is difficult to trace on Long Mountain as much of it is covered with modern tree plantation, landscaping, tracks and a water system for the Leighton Hall estate. As it enters the estate it climbs steeply alongside the modern road until it moves to hold a line on approximately the 275m contour just above a steeper slope. Here the line of the Dyke curves with the contour until it appears to run directly across less steep ground to cross a small stream that has been much dammed to create a series of pools. Beyond this point there are several earthworks on Moel y Mab (SJ 250 055), but that on the lower edge of the wood, near Pentre, is in line with the Dyke that is clearly defined to the north. The reason for the sudden change in the alignment to run up onto the higher ground of Long Mountain is not easy to explain. A lower route across the foot of Long Mountain at about the 170m contour would seem more direct and would reach Pentre at about the 130m contour. There is only one minor stream crossing this line and so the avoidance of watercourses seems unlikely to be the answer and the views to the west are still good from the lower level, the River Severn being about 100m above sea level at this point. All the normal explanations do not seem to fit the circumstances here and the question must be asked as to whether the upstanding banks visible today are in fact Offa's Dyke or whether some are earlier or later banks. It has not been possible to carry out extensive research in this area as it is not only part of a private estate but is also heavily wooded. From Pentre, the line of Offa's Dyke can be traced across the agricultural landscape in an almost straight line until it reaches the modern road just to the south of Buttington.

Site 46, Redwood Lodge, Buttington (SJ 249 081)
An excavation here confirmed that the full 2m-deep ditch had been part of the original construction on this straight lowland length. Although the bank was denuded, a distinct layer of stone was to be seen at the base of the bank (23).

From the point where Offa's Dyke meets the modern road, just to the south of the Old School House at Buttington, it is lost for 7km (about 4 miles) on the floodplain until it can be seen again on the west side of the River Severn near Llandrinio (site 200).

Fox had suggested that the line had followed the west side of a boundary hedge in the field across the road from the Old School House at Buttington and had then left the hedge to cross the field on a heading that would take it directly to the River Severn. The evidence 7km downstream does suggest that the Dyke coming across the floodplain from the north did approach the River Severn directly. Thus, if the Dyke coming from the south also crossed the river directly, one of two hypotheses might be suggested: firstly that there had been no built earthwork as the River Severn was seen as a sufficient barrier or, secondly, that the Dyke had been built throughout the entire 7km but on the west bank of the river. The first suggestion seems unlikely because the river is easily fordable in a number of places. The second suggestion is, in some respects, even more unlikely, as, in terms of a defensive line or even a defensible one, an earthwork with a ditch to

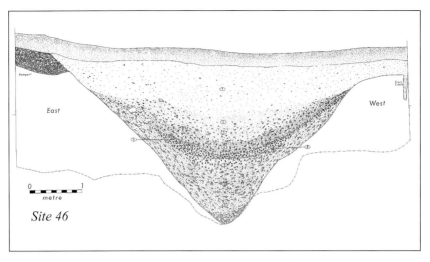

23 *Section drawing of V-shaped ditch at Redwood Lodge, Powys (SJ 249 084). Note the use of flat stone to consolidate the base of the bank at this point*

the west and a major river almost immediately behind it does not seem to make good strategic sense.

Our observations in other areas of how sensitive the line taken by the Dyke was to local topography whilst keeping a defensible line and views to the west suggested a third possibility, that the Dyke did not cross the river near Buttington but continued to hold the higher ground of the old river terrace on which the church stands, and from there continued along the eastern side of the river until it was opposite the next known length on the west bank. Our recent research therefore has concentrated on this area with five excavations, four of which took place in the area on the west side of the Buttington to Leighton road.

Site 181, Cletterwood, Buttington (SJ 249 085)

A slight bank and ditch along a hedge line offered a possible continuation, just across the road from where the Dyke is last seen on the east side of the road near the Old School House. Fox had thought the Dyke continued on this line, but the upstanding remains on the eastern side of the hedge proved to be the upcast of the last two centuries from the cleaning out of a small stream that used to flow in the adjacent ditch. An extension of this excavation on the western side of the hedge did show an area of compacted clay close to the surface and a resistivity survey traced this for some distance along the western side of the field boundary. The Ordnance Survey maps show a discontinuous bank crossing the field from this hedge although no such features are visible at the surface today. The geophysical survey was extended to this area and a distinct anomaly was found indicating the possibility of some buried remains of the bank seen by Fox.

The area of the floodplain at Buttington has a very complex depositional history with at least two former channels of the River Severn crossing the field that we were investigating and silts up to several metres deep as the present river channel is approached. The most western trench (site 206, Buttington, Cropmark, SJ 248 086), that is the one closest to the river, was sited across the former bank, seen by Fox crossing the field and marked on the Ordnance Survey map and the geophysical anomaly. This long trench gave us a view of the complex sequence of river deposits but although there were many different contexts present, after careful examination, none were considered to be archaeological. The trench was therefore recorded and backfilled.

Site 205, Buttington, Hedgeline (SJ 249 085)

The excavation was located in relation to the geophysical survey near the hedge and to site 181. The earlier excavation had revealed what appeared to be the remains of the eastern side of a clay bank and site 205 was therefore located over what was expected to be the position of the western side of this bank, based on the normal width of the bank of Offa's Dyke. Such a clay bank with stones was located and seemed to be beginning to drop down towards the west, although the sequence was interrupted by a modern field drain. This work was carried out by hand, but it was clear that if a 2m-deep ditch on the scale of Offa's Dyke was present it would need to be excavated by machine. This was done and the sections and floor cleaned. A complex series of deposits was revealed but no clear evidence for a ditch. The layers seemed to represent phases of water-laid deposits and included an area containing macroscopic plant remains including hazelnut shells. The whole sequence was up to 2m deep and was laid down above natural clay that was a surprisingly bright blue in colour.

The decision was then taken to remove the bank end of the trench to the same depth as the west end. Initially this appeared to show only naturally deposited layers. However, after careful cleaning and identification of the various contexts for the section drawing, it could be seen that the natural layers that underlay the clay bank had been interrupted and that a disturbed or mixed deposit was to the west of this with a shallow cut into the blue clay at its base that could not have been made by natural processes. The western side of this feature was more difficult to determine but seemed to butt up to the organic material. It is possible that this feature represents a ditch, the clay with stones at the most easterly end representing the remains of a bank with material from it spread towards the west when the bank was pushed over, an event that we know to have taken place after the time of Fox's description. The evidence now points to this being a continuation of Offa's Dyke, the course of which is clear only 200 yards to the south. The bank is on the edge of the old river terrace and so the construction of the Dyke has been modified to accommodate the wet ground that it encountered on the floodplain.

Site 208, Buttington, Field Gate (SJ 249 084)

A third trench (site 208) to the south of site 205 showed a similar natural depositional phase as that in site 205, but was probably too far west to pick up evidence of a similar archaeological sequence, if such exists here.

The three excavations seem to indicate that there is some evidence for Offa's Dyke continuing along the river terrace that forms the eastern boundary of this field but that it does not cross the field on a line that would take it to the bank of the River Severn, *contra* Fox's suggestion. This would allow the Dyke to hold the drier, higher ground and to continue along the east bank of the River Severn before crossing to Llandrinio where it is next seen on the west side of the river some distance downstream.

Site 207, Trewern, Old Mills (SJ 275 127)

The fourth trench in the season of investigations on the floodplain was located at Mills Moat, some distance along the eastern bank of the River Severn and just above the present flood line. It was excavated by hand to a depth that clearly indicated that, although there had been disturbance consistent with the pushing over of a bank, there was no ditch present and therefore the former bank had not been the remains of Offa's Dyke. The site was recorded and backfilled mechanically with the considerable and very welcome help of the landowner!

Thus our knowledge has moved forward, albeit in negatives in three trenches. We can now be reasonably sure that the Dyke did not cross the Severn at Buttington but continued on the east bank ,although we have still not located it along the bank of the Severn between here and Llandrinio and more fieldwork is needed before further excavation can be considered.

Site 45, Burnt Lane, Trewern (SJ 264 110) CPAT

This earlier excavation on the eastern side of the river between site 205 and 207 found no evidence for any bank earlier than the modern, nineteenth-century, flood banks and no ditch was observed in the pipe trench approaching the flood bank. This was a watching brief carried out by Chris Musson of Clwyd-Powys Archaeological Trust during the laying of a gas pipeline through the flood bank. This site, however, is below the modern flood line and any continuation of Offa's Dyke along the eastern bank of the River Severn might be expected to be on slightly higher ground.

This may be the only length of Offa's Dyke to run along the course of a significant river. There is a question as to whether a short length of the River Dee is utilised further north and this is discussed below. Where the Dyke approached the Camlad as it leaves the Montgomery Plain and to the north, the Vyrnwy near Llanymynech, it does so almost at right angles and the evidence from sites 117 and 118 discussed above suggest that it was built right up to the banks of the Camlad.

To the north of the River Severn the situation is rather clearer, particularly since the 1996 excavations by Engineering Archaeological Services at Rhyd Esgyn, Llandrinio (site 200, SJ 282 155). The National Rivers Authority planned to rebuild one of the flood banks and, prior to their work, an archaeological excavation was carried out on the presumed line of Offa's Dyke. This showed that the old flood bank covered an earlier low bank and to the west of this early bank was a ditch of Offan proportions. Radiocarbon dating of wood samples from the ditch showed that it had been open as late as the fifteenth century but no dating for the building of the dyke was obtained. It does, however, confirm that the short length of bank that runs at right angles to the river and the flood defence bank is in fact a part of Offa's Dyke. This bank stands to within 50m of the present north bank of the River Severn.

The bank at Rhyd Esgyn is in line with the evidence found at The Nea, Llandrinio (site 44, SJ 276 163) where a rescue excavation was carried out in advance of the laying of a gas pipeline across the lane and a U-shaped ditch 5m wide and more than 1.5m deep was recorded. This is consistent with the scale of the ditch on Offa's Dyke.

From Llandrinio the line of the Dyke runs in straight alignments to the River Vyrnwy at Llanymynech. The ground between Llandrinio and Four Crosses is relatively flat and has drainage channels and flood defences in many parts. It is, however, a landscape of farms and rich grazing land and there is visible evidence for Offa's Dyke in a number of places.

The presence of Offa's Dyke was confirmed at site 21, Four Crosses, Llandysilio (SJ 271 183). As the village of Four Crosses is approached, Offa's Dyke is cut by a now disused railway, and a section was cut across the bank and ditch adjacent to the railway. The base of the bank was intact, no old ground surface was recognised and the natural deposits below the bank were stones in clay, typical glacial deposits in this lowland context. The bank was made up of a basal layer consisting of sandy clay with occasional stones and overlaid with clay with some stone. There appeared to be a layer of material redeposited from the bank over the ditch but below this was a fine silty fill. The ditch was over 1m deep and 4.5m wide; that is similar to that excavated at The Nea. Beneath the bank was found evidence of the Neolithic pit alignment located and excavated elsewhere by Clwyd-Powys Archaeological Trust and the Dyke intersects the Neolithic pit alignment at this point.

Cambrian Archaeological Projects observed the excavation of foundations for a property being built on the southern edge of the village of Four Crosses. Although there was no surface evidence for Offa's Dyke at this point, it was on the presumed line. The excavation exposed the eroded base of the bank of Offa's Dyke that survived to almost a metre high but completely below the present ground level.

The bank is to be seen beside to the main A483 road through Four Crosses and the ditch was observed in a small roadworks excavation outside the former entrance to the school. At the north end of this village the road bends slightly to the east as it moves onto the floodplain of the River Vyrnwy and crosses the river within a deep meander. The exact position of Offa's Dyke in this section is not certain. It is next certainly identified on the south-western end of Llanymynech Hill. The direct route between these two points would take it across the River Vyrnwy to the west of the modern road and bridge. Whilst this seems a reasonable crossing point, it does lead into a very wet area of the flood plain whereas the village of Llanymynech is on higher ground. If the Dyke crossed the river on the approximate line of the modern road it would have only a narrow strip of wet ground to cross to each side of the river. One opinion is that the road is on the course of the Dyke and that it turns up the slope of Llanymynech Hill only at the northern end of the village. Another opinion is that, having crossed the river successfully, it then takes a more direct course up onto the western side of the hill. Both postulated routes would arrive on the flatter area at the top of the hill near Asterley Rocks (**24**) and this brings us into the third zone through which the Dyke passes.

24 *Asterley Rocks are at the western end of Llanymynech Hill where Offa's Dyke can be seen after the crossing of the River Vyrnwy (see* **22***)*

Llanymynech to Treuddyn (25)

The third zone, north of the River Vyrnwy, is in one respect different
from all of Offa's Dyke to the south in that it marks the edge of a topographical zone, rather than crossing one. This northern section runs
along the edge of the Welsh uplands, above the Shropshire/Cheshire
plain. The line that Offa's Dyke follows in this section is more complex
and intricate than further south as the terrain is cut by the valleys of
many streams and rivers. However, the line is still primarily a series
of straight alignments that dominate the view to the west. What on
a modern map may look a poor line is shown to be a careful choice
when the topography is examined on the ground. The earthwork passes
through the village of Llanfynydd, as it turned towards Treuddyn, in a
close and complex countryside of small valleys and little streams. The
road to Treuddyn is on the bank of the Dyke with the clearly defined
and considerable ditch to its south-west. All signs of the bank and the
ditch are lost at SJ 268 577. This terminus is short of the valley of the
River Alyn, a tributary of the River Dee, and a long way short of the
sea or the Dee estuary.

To return to the detailed line, after leaving the floodplain of the
River Vyrnwy and reaching Asterley Rocks, we find that the situation
on Llanymynech Hill is complicated by the fact that in the eighth
century this had already had an Iron Age hillfort constructed on it,
and the bank of both the hillfort and the Dyke would seem to sit on
the edge of the steep northern side of the hill. In places this is almost a
sheer rockface. Mining has taken place on top of the hill from at least
Roman times and there has been extensive quarrying of the limestone.
The quarries are, however, mainly on the southern side of the hill and
all the evidence points to the western side being in its natural state.
The hilltop is today a golf course, which does limit its potential for
archaeological investigation. The hillfort is bounded at its eastern end
by three banks and ditches that cross a narrow neck of land. East of this
point, the bank of Offa's Dyke along Blodwel Rocks and Llynclys Hill
is not entirely clear but it is certainly not the north-east-facing rectilinear enclosure bank that was identified as Offa's Dyke by Cyril Fox.
Air photographs have shown this enclosure to contain circular features
consistent with Iron Age huts and it appears to be an occupied area
outside the main Iron Age fortification. What is certain is that Offa's

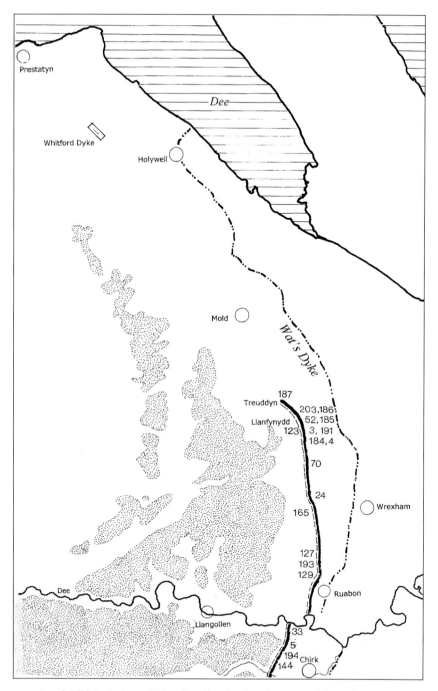

25 *Map of Offa's Dyke from Chirk to Treuddyn showing sites excavated. The relative situation of Offa's Dyke to Wat's Dyke, Whitford Dyke and the coast is also shown*

Dyke descends from Llynclys Hill and is clearly visible to the rear of the Old School House at Porth y waen.

Site 22, Porth y waen, Oswestry (SJ 271 239)
There is clear indication of the bank and ditch descending from Llynclys Hill at this point and the excavation revealed a considerable ditch.

The line of the Dyke disappears under the Old School House and the modern road. Its line is also missing for the next kilometre as extensive mining at Whitehaven Quarry has removed all evidence. There had already been extensive limestone extraction prior to Fox's inventory and the first edition large-scale Ordnance Survey maps give little help. However, Fox noted that the parish boundary follows a line round the contour of the hill that would join with the next visible section of upstanding Dyke on Blodwel Bank. This seems a likely explanation, as the line of Offa's Dyke is the national and parish boundary on Llanymynech Hill, the parish boundary on Blodwel Rocks and again on Blodwel Bank. However, the combination of quarrying and mineral railway lines on the north side of the valley renders any hope of finding a trace of the Dyke impossible.

The line between Asterley Rocks and Blodwel Bank is a considerable deviation from the direct line and needs some explanation. Llanymynech Hill commands views west over the confluence of the River Tanat with the River Vyrnwy and south across the floodplain of the River Severn. The main valley of the River Tanat turns from a west/east line to a north/south line to curve round the southern foot of Llanymynech Hill. The north-western slopes of Llanymynech Hill and Blodwel Rocks, on which the Dyke is situated, look across a steep-sided, flat-bottomed side valley that is marshy in parts, open at its western end but almost closed at its eastern end. A consideration of this narrow opening at the eastern end suggests that it is original and is not a result of quarrying. The Dyke is clearly visible descending from Llynclys Hill to the valley bottom (site 22) on the south side and must have climbed up the north side to where it can still be seen on Blodwel Bank. It would seem unlikely that this would be the case if the cliffs had been continuous to form a blind end to the valley in the eighth century. If there had been a high level link between the southern and northern sides of the valley, all need to descend to the valley floor would have been obviated.

We still need to consider why the planners of the Dyke did not follow a direct line across the western mouth of this side valley. Such a direct course would have meant giving up some of the advantage of the views to the west and the ground crossed would have been marshy. There is also the advantage of the existing bank of the Iron Age hillfort along Llanymynech Hill and the need for only a slight earthwork along the sheer edge of Blodwel Rock. Perhaps more importantly, the siting of the Dyke across the narrow eastern entrance to the valley controls a route that gives access to central Wales as the Tanat Valley leads over a pass to Bala and the Vyrnwy Valley to Meifod and Mathrafal; three centres of royal power of the kings of Gwynedd and Powys in the early medieval period.

North from Blodwel Bank, the line is again clear with upstanding bank for much of the length through the villages of Treflach and Trefonen, holding a straight line that occasionally has a slightly restricted view to the west. Where there is higher ground to the west, the dead ground is covered by the views from north and south. It is also a line that avoids a number of small tributary streams and is on the best line it can take on the watershed. It crosses a minor stream at Trefonen and drops down into the steep-sided valley of the River Morda at Candy Mill. It crosses the Morda just after it has turned onto a west/east course and then the Dyke holds the valley side where the river runs north/south. The construction of the Dyke on the valley side is less substantial than on the lowlands of the central zone or where it is climbing hills and descending valleys in the southern zone. The slope of the valley side is used, cut back to make it steeper and with a slight bank on the uphill side and another on the downhill side, giving it the appearance of a considerable earthwork with a deep ditch. Archaeologically this makes it difficult to identify where it does not remain as a visible earthwork as there has been very little alteration to the natural slope of the ground and no deep ditch was excavated as part of the original construction.

The Dyke runs through Racecourse Wood and again dominates the view to the west as it skirts the nineteenth-century Oswestry Racecourse and moves slightly to the west to curve round the forward slope of Baker's Hill, which it crosses in its fully built form of bank and deep ditch. Mortimer Wheeler reported on an excavation along this section in 1922, when a length of ditch was emptied of its silts in the area of SJ 25 31 (numbered in our sequence as site 69). Wheeler's report in the 1923 Bulletin of the Board of Celtic Studies, which was its first volume, is worth noting:

> A society, known as the Oswestry Prehistoric Society, has been formed, largely on the initiative of Mr Northcote W. Thomas of Trefonen, near Oswestry, Lord Harlech is the first president. The society is established with the excellent purpose of exploring and surveying Offa's Dyke. Some thirty yards of the ditch was excavated just south of a gap on Baker's Hill (Shrop. Xi, E.E.) in lat. 52 degrees 52'32", but the only finds were a flint chip, possibly artificial, and a fragment of thick, coarsely glazed pottery. Not much local support was forthcoming, and as it was desirable to arouse local interest, another item on the programme was attacked and the main work this season has been the exploratory excavations in the earthworks of Old Oswestry.

It is worth noting that Cyril Fox was appointed Keeper of Archaeology at the National Museum of Wales in 1925, the Director being Mortimer Wheeler who greeted him with the news that he was to receive 'sufficient annual leave of absence for fieldwork' on Offa's Dyke. Fox began this work in 1926 and completed it in the summer of 1931. Fox also decided that excavation was not as informative as he had hoped. We can confirm the lack of artefactual evidence from excavation but our understanding of the line and structure of Offa's Dyke has gained enormously from our own numerous excavations and detailed surveys.

From Baker's Hill, the line drops down to Carreg-y-big where the bank was recorded in advance of the construction of a silage pit.

Site 74, Carreg-y-big, Selattyn (SJ 253 323)
The remains of the original bank were less substantial than had appeared from the surface as there was upcast, probably from the cleaning out of a nearby drainage ditch, on the eastern side. Beneath this and to the west, the original bank remained to a height of 1.5m and a minimum of 5.5m in width; the front of the bank and its relationship with the ditch was not explored, as it was not a part of the necessary cut for the silage pit.

Towards the front of the bank a low mound of yellow clay with stone was interpreted as a marking out bank.

The Dyke continues north, climbing the hill from Carreg-y-big towards Orseddwen on a straight alignment. It curves slightly to cross a small stream in a deep dingle, and appears to curve at Orseddwen Farm before moving towards the west slightly and then east to take the forward slope round Selattyn Hill and down into the deep valley at Craignant.

Site 29, Orseddwyn, Selattyn (SJ 251 339)
This excavation was carried out to investigate a site that Fox had described as a possible original gateway, although his published photograph would seem to show a remnant of lowered bank across the gap. Our excavation found the remains of the bank, the ditch and a low counterscarp bank to the west. These low banks on the western lip of the ditch are an occasional feature of the Dyke's construction, particularly when it is running directly up and down hills. It may be that the shallow soils made excavation of a full-scale ditch more difficult and so a small western bank gives the appearance of a deeper ditch. It must be said, however, that in places the ditch has been cut through bedrock and there may have been other reasons for these counterscarp banks, but as no evidence has been found for re-cutting or cleaning out of the ditch that might have resulted in such a bank, we consider them to be part of the original plan. In any event, such a bank is visible as a surface feature on the hill between Carreg-y-big and Orseddwyn. The excavation showed clearly that this was not an original gap as all elements of the earthwork were found. One point of interest here was that the ditch (just under 1m deep) appeared to be shallow in relation to the size of the bank adjacent to the gap. Stones up to 50cm in diameter were found in the base of the ditch and in the counterscarp bank. Much large stone is visible at the surface along this length of the Dyke, particularly on the western side. However, when the excavation was in progress, the farmer informed us that these were not found within the fields when he ploughed them. The explanation may be that some material was imported to the site to build the main bank that still stands to more than 3.5m in places and the material for which could not have been derived solely from the ditch.

Site 63, Woodside, Selattyn (SJ 251 346)

The opportunity was taken to record a partial section of bank exposed during rebuilding operations to the south of a cottage that cuts into the eastern edge of the bank. Approximately half of the width of the bank standing to a height of 1m above the old ground level was exposed at this time. A layer of large stones was observed at the base of the bank with a layer of hard-packed clay with some stone overlying it and with the whole of the exposed part of the bank covered by a layer of looser clayey material.

The sides of the Craignant Valley are steep but the line is direct except for a slight diversion to the east to avoid the confluence of two streams. From the plateau above the north side of Craignant, Offa's Dyke trends to the east and as the Ceiriog Valley is approached, the views to the west open up and are spectacular in places. A long, and in places steep, stretch down to the River Ceiriog has good upstanding bank and ditch remaining for much of its length. The Dyke is, however, lost in the valley bottom in the modern road system. It reappears at the top of the wood on the north side of the valley above Castle Mill and from there follows a straight line through the grounds of Chirk Castle. Although it is much reduced in size in some parts of the parkland, it was left intact when the ornamental lakes were created and the bank can be seen just above or just below the surface depending on the water level. An excavation within the parkland by C.J. Arnold *(pers comm)* in 1991 recorded that although there was no upstanding bank in an access gap, the ditch was present below ground and the bank had been removed in the nineteenth century.

The earthwork is then visible for most of the next length until it begins to drop down in the Vale of Llangollen and reaches the main road, beyond which a footpath marks its course until a short length is visible between the Llangollen canal and the River Dee.

Site 144, Home Farm, Chirk Castle (SJ 267 383) CPAT

Clwyd-Powys Archaeological Trust reported their findings at this site in *Archaeology in Wales* (Volume 28) as follows:

> A watching brief was undertaken during the laying of a new water main across a section of Offa's Dyke near Chirk Castle in February 1988 (SJ 2675 3835). A machine-dug trench *c.*0.5m

wide and up to 2.0m deep afforded a reasonably clear but oblique section across the dyke. Prior to the work a contour survey of the site was produced. The exposed section revealed a buried soil *c*.4cm thick underlying the bank, a sample of which produced no environmental or dating evidence after flotation. The main bank material consisted of redeposited natural clay, presumably upcast from the ditch, surviving to no more than 1.0m above the buried soil. The bank at this point was *c*.3.0m wide. The trench was not sufficiently deep to record a profile of the ditch or its width, although there appeared to be a narrow berm *c*.0.8m wide between the bank and the lip of the ditch.

Site 5, Caeau-Gwynion, Chirk (SJ 273 395) Fox
This site was excavated by Fox in 1928 with a view to determining the original depth and form of the ditch. The published report states:

> The ditch was found to be flat-floored, 6.5ft in breadth on the floor and about 18ft in breadth at ground level; the depth of the silting varies from 3ft 9in to 4ft 10in . . . The line of the original ground level was determined by excavation in the scarp and reverse slope of the bank; this enabled the original maximum depth of the ditch to be fixed, within narrow limits of error, at 7.7ft. The bank was composed of gravely and sandy clay, the ditch silt of similar material overlaid by a considerable depth of fine soil. (Fox, page 70)

It is interesting that Fox should have chosen a site where the bank and ditch face uphill, an unusual situation along the course of the entire Dyke.

Site 33, Plas Offa, Chirk (SJ 282 406)
At this site, a cut end of the bank was cleaned and recorded. The bank consisted of a series of layers, mainly of clay with some stone and gravel. There was evidence for the whole bank having been stabilised with turf, at least some of which had been removed from the area under the bank prior to it being built.

The north bank of the River Dee, which forms a considerable barrier, shows no evidence for the bank or ditch, but the line becomes clear again about 2km to the north on the outskirts of Ruabon. If a direct line is taken between the last sighting to the south and the next north it would suggest that it would have curved round the forward slope of the small hill on which Cefn Wood is situated today. This line would keep the western slope and views and would avoid several small tributary steams of the River Dee. The area between the River Dee and Ruabon has been much disturbed by the railway, by mining, quarrying, tile and brick works and woodland. Fox examined a suggested line to Home Farm where traces of a possible ditch can be seen to the west of the farm track and in a small wood when the track trends in a more easterly direction. Further south, the line favoured by Fox is along the edge of the steep valley of one of these side streams although he found the evidence less convincing as the River Dee is approached. This would bring the Dyke to the River Dee some distance downstream (east) from its last sighting on the south bank.

Fox appears to have considered an alternative line and noted that Lewis' *Topographical Dictionary*, published in 1833, stated that the Dyke left Wynnstay Park 'near the Waterloo Tower' above Cefn railway station. This would fit well with a direct line north from the crossing of the River Dee and with a line curving round Cefn Wood hill. Fox discounted this line as he could see no surface evidence. Offa's Dyke Project carried out resistivity survey and fieldwork in the area of the Waterloo Tower and Cefn Wood, but failed to find any evidence for the Dyke here. The line along Home Farm Lane and through Hopyard Wood has not been tested by excavation. This line would make the River Dee the defensive line for a short distance, which, if true, could have implications for the situation on the River Severn near Buttington (discussed above) although the break in the known Dyke on the River Severn is much longer.

The line through Ruabon, despite modern industrial and urban disturbance, has survived remarkably well. It still stands to a good height with a considerable ditch to the south of the schools, and is alongside the road almost as far as the road between Ruabon and Johnstown. It is then present either under or adjacent to this road through Johnstown, but follows a more directly northern line to skirt the western summit of a small hill when the road turns to the north-west. The Dyke is visible on the hill and drops down to cross the Pentrebychan Brook at a point below the confluence of the brook with two smaller streams and continues in a direct line to cross the River Clwydog. This straight line continues through the much-disturbed area of Brymbo surviving on the western edge of the opencast workings. It emerges beyond the built-up area, still following this direct line, until it crosses the River Alyn and curves westward following the valley side. The line is on the east side of the valley, keeping the view to the west, and the valley road follows the same course. The dyke continues to the village of Llanfynydd and then crosses the little valley at Pantystain to follow the ridge up the hill towards Treuddyn. Here the ditch is more marked and, as at Llanfynydd, the road is built on top of the bank. The Dyke would appear to end at SJ 268 577.

The modern landscape through which Offa's Dyke passes from the River Dee to its northern terminus is very different from that to the south. The extensive industrial activity for much of this length should not distract us from the principles of its layout that were observed in the less disturbed areas. Its course is direct but sensitive to contours and to river crossings and it keeps a good view to the west wherever possible. If one attempts to ignore the modern and concentrate on the natural topography, it can be seen that these principles are followed throughout the entire length from Rushock Hill to Treuddyn.

A number of excavations have confirmed the line and structure of the bank and ditch north of the River Dee.

Site 129, Tatham Road, Ruabon (SJ302 448)

An excavation was carried out at this site in advance of the development of an area of wasteland. The land was situated in the angle at the end of the lane from Ruabon, which has good bank alongside it, and the main Ruabon to Johnstown Road. The known line through Johnstown suggested that Offa's Dyke would have taken a more northerly line before this road junction and indeed the excavation confirmed this as no trace of bank or ditch were found.

Site 127, Harrington's Caravans, Johnstown (SJ 300 457)

The former caravan sales site was due to be redeveloped for a supermarket and car park and the excavation was carried out in advance of this work. Evidence was found for the structure of the western face of the bank, part of which was made up of turfs. The eastern part of the bank had been covered by the modern road and some modern build up of land to the east of the Dyke would have been necessary to accommodate the full width of the modern road. The natural level of the ground on the eastern side of the road is below the present road level. On the western side of the road there is a steeper slope down and although the area within the caravan sales site had been levelled, the excavation showed that this slope was the bank of Offa's Dyke and that the ditch was below the level of the modern surface. It was not possible to fully excavate the ditch area, as it was unstable through water seepage.

Site 193, Ruabon Road, Johnstown (SJ 301 455) Earthworks

Our excavation in Johnstown was carried out in 1986, and in 1996 Earthworks carried out a watching brief in advance of housing development. The levelling of the ground to provide access from the main road to the east of the line of the Dyke was the main disturbance likely to reveal evidence but none was found. Their conclusion was that the bank was under the road at this point, although our evidence from Tatham Road and Harrington's would suggest that it was within the site but had probably been destroyed some years earlier when the area was levelled for its former industrial use. The evidence for any ditch was not investigated.

Site 165, Esclusham (SJ 298 484) CPAT

A machine-cut trench through a scheduled section of Offa's Dyke for a gas pipeline was observed and recorded at this site. The cleaned section showed a bank of dump construction 8m wide and remaining to a height of 1.5m. A 5m-wide ditch, 2m deep, was also observed but this had had a modern field-ditch and a drain set into it making any information about the original fill of the ditch of Offa's Dyke difficult to record.

Site 24, Coedpoeth (SJ 293 512)

This excavation was carried out for the Department of the Environment in advance of sewer trenching. This allowed a 10m section across the Dyke to be examined which showed that a turf stack had formed a substantial part of the bank. Below the bank, and following its line, was a shallow 1.5m-wide ditch filled with large stones. A small bank ran alongside this feature to its east. These were interpreted as a marking out feature dug to show the line the full-sized earthwork was to take.

Site 70, Brymbo area (SJ 29 52) McKenny Hughes

Excavation was carried out in the area of Brymbo in 1892 by Professor T. McKenny Hughes who was concerned to find whether the ditch was present where it could not be seen on the ground. He recognised that where it was to be seen it was on the western side and that the bank was also normally steeper on this side. He records that he 'dug at the base of the vallum [bank] in one or two places near Brymbo, and examined it carefully in other parts of the line' but 'was unable to make out that there ever had been a fosse [ditch] at the bottom of the vallum'. On his published figures, which are not records of sections cut but diagrams to show his thesis, he indicates that he could have been excavating under the former bank. These explorations add nothing to our knowledge of the Dyke, but they do represent the earliest known attempt to answer specific questions about Offa's Dyke by excavation. Fortunately later fieldworkers have had greater success.

Site 4, Ffrith Hall (SJ 288 548) Fox

This was another excavation by Cyril Fox in 1927, which, in conjunction with site 3 (opposite) was designed to ascertain whether Offa's Dyke was built before or after the Roman occupation. He reports on his work as follows:

> The only point reasonably close to Ffrith village where the Dyke was undamaged save by time and of characteristic profile, was at Ffrith Hall, 470 yards to the south-east and it was thought worthwhile to test the Dyke here for the presence of Roman remains . . . a trench was dug through the rampart; its maximum height above ancient ground level was shown to be 6ft 8in, and the existence of the ditch on the west side thereof proven. No artefacts of any sort were found; the site is evidently well outside the [Roman] settlement area.

Site 184, Sunnybank, Ffrith (SJ 285 552) CPAT
A rescue excavation was funded by Cadw and carried out by CPAT
in 1990 in advance of building work at this property. This was within
the area of known Roman activity and on the line of Offa's Dyke.
The excavation showed that the bank survived here to a height of
0.8m above the old ground surface and was composed of successive dumps of silty clay with angular stone. One of the lower levels,
containing large stones, also contained a 'significant quantity' of
Roman pottery that confirmed Fox's dating for the Roman settlement of late first to mid-second century AD. There was a partial
excavation of the material below the bank and an old ground surface
was identified. This was a 12cm-thick layer of dark grey clay silt and
pottery from this layer also contained Roman material, including a
sherd of Samian ware datable to between AD 160 and 190. Below
the old ground surface, more second-century Roman pottery was
found and below that, compacted stone that could have been a road
or hard standing.

Site 3, Ffrith Village (SJ 284 553) Fox
Another Fox excavation from 1927 in which he examined a stretch of
bank close to the post office. The site was close to the known Roman
buildings in the area and therefore considered to be a good place to
examine the relationship between Offa's Dyke and Roman remains.
The excavation was limited to the west by the presence of the roadside
wall, then in poor condition at this point. The crest of the bank was
considered to have been reached but was not excavated down to the
old ground surface west of this point because of the danger of the
wall collapsing. To the east, the old ground surface was exposed for
about 25ft. At the crest, 5ft of bank remained and was shown to be
made of a core of water-worn boulders with black, charcoal-stained,
soil between and over them. Above this was a layer of stony clay with
dark patches among it. The whole was covered with a thick layer
of humus. Throughout the bank, numerous fragments of Roman
pottery, none later than the second century AD and including sherds
of Samian ware were found together with a bronze rivet and one
piece of glass.

Fox describes how the subsoil below the bank was carefully
examined. Charcoal was found in the upper layers of subsoil and

two shallow scoops in it also contained charcoal. In one, three worn sherds of pottery were found, and in the other a fragment of tile. Fox concluded that the bank material included some derived from Roman rubbish pits. To the west of these and further under the standing bank of Offa's Dyke was a 1ft 8in-diameter posthole. The top of the hole had three water-worn boulders blocking it, there was no trace of any decayed wood and indeed the posthole was completely empty. Fox suggested that this hole had contained a post, wedged in place with stones, before the bank had been built and that the post had been withdrawn immediately before the bank was built, leaving the stones blocking the hole. This post, if Fox's interpretation is correct, could represent an alternative method of marking out the proposed line of the Dyke. There must be some hesitation about this conclusion as unpublished photographs of the excavation show that it was not carried out to modern standards, being excavated by workmen with Fox only present on site from time to time. The posthole was only observed below the old ground surface, but the method of excavation would have been unlikely to reveal any evidence at a higher level. An examination of the published section shows the position of the post as being immediately to the east of the stones that made up the base of the bank and therefore the extraction of the post and the deposition of the stones in its mouth could seem to fit with a stage when the bank had been partially built.

Fox's suggested chronology for this site was that the evidence of the Roman remains indicated that the bank could not have been dug before AD 200 and probably later than AD 400. He also noted that it was not modern and therefore nothing had been found to contradict the traditional dating to the reign of Offa. He also considered that the charcoal-filled hollows might have been contemporary with the build of the Dyke and the abraded Roman sherds within them as residual. Excavated before the advent of radiocarbon dating, it was of course not possible to be certain on this point. The section drawing also shows finds of Roman date at points below the stone core of the bank and below the old ground surface. This seems to suggest that there was a period of time between the deposition of the Roman material and the building of the bank during which the ground surface was created. However, as the posthole and the two scoops are all shown in the section together with numerous find spots, it is likely that this is a composite section rather than an accurate drawing of a single side of the trench. Therefore, the finds below the dark line indicating the ground surface may in fact have been within it.

Site 191, Ffrith Farm (SJ 285 553) Earthworks

An excavation here by Earthworks in 1995 in advance of housing development found a mixed upper layer with fragments of modern material, Roman roof tile and a worked flint, probably of the Neolithic period. This was a single layer and although much of the material was found in the upper level of the layer and could be contamination from the layer above, this was not true for all of the artefacts. This layer sealed a wide, shallow ditch (8-10m wide and 1m deep) that was considered to be that of Offa's Dyke. The feature could not be fully investigated as it was partly below a hedge and outside the area available for investigation. This site was close to Fox's excavations and the finds of Roman building material were to be expected. Their position suggests disturbance, perhaps from the building of Offa's Dyke and its later destruction.

Site 123, Coed Isa, Llanfynydd (SJ 282 562)

This was an observation made during the removal of part of the surfacing of the road at a point where the ditch, and possibly part of the bank, should have been under the road. The material exposed below the road surfacing was not natural geology, but other than this no further information could be gleaned.

Site 52, Schoolfield, Llanfynydd (SJ 279 567)

This site revealed a considerable ditch approximately 4m wide at ground level (the western lip of the ditch was not within the excavated area) and 1.5m deep. The ground rose steeply to the east but only a short length of turf and topsoil was removed beyond the eastern lip of the ditch, and the bank was not excavated. The primary silting of the ditch consisted of freestone that seemed to have tumbled down the bank and therefore could be interpreted as evidence for a drystone wall on top of the bank (**26**).

Two excavations were carried out in Llanfynydd in 1998 by Earthworks, one to the north and one to the south of our site 52 (site 185, SJ 279 565 and site 186, SJ 277 568). The one to the north revealed a well-preserved section of the Dyke measuring 15m wide

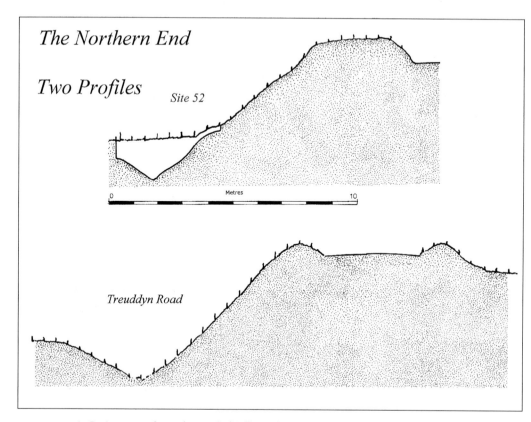

26 *Sections across the northern end of Offa's Dyke at Llanfynydd and Treuddyn has the modern road on top of the bank (as at Johnstown, site 127) but the ditch to the west can be clearly seen*

and about 1m high with a western ditch (site 186). In 1999 Clwyd-Powys Archaeological Trust carried out a watching brief during the laying of foundations and service trenches alongside the road and observed a partially collapsed bank on the western side of the road that suggested that it was the remains of Offa's Dyke (site 203, SJ 277 569).

The most northerly reported excavation of Offa's Dyke was where Clwyd-Powys Archaeological Trust excavated at Coed Talon, Treuddyn (site 187, SJ 2672 5773). They reported in *Archaeology of Wales* that a watching brief was carried out at this site in 1989. The brief report records that the observations were made during the replacement of crash barriers along the B5101, which they reported to be on top of the bank of Offa's Dyke at this point. Because of the nature of the work, two longitudinal sections were cut by machine, one about 175m long and the other about 135m long and each up to 1.5m deep. Their conclusion was that, 'These revealed the upper part of the bank which was composed of yellow stony clay and indicated that the bank had been widened at this point to accommodate the road [in modern times]'.

After the Dyke reaches the area of the defunct railway at Pantystain Crossing and has crossed the Afon Cegidog, the ditch is clearly visible to the north for a distance of about half a kilometre to a point where a lane turns down to Tan-llan. Although no excavation has been undertaken to the north of the Afon Cegidog, we believe that the conclusion of this feature marks the northern termination. The oft-repeated remark that the dyke ends at Treuddyn Chapel depends on a misreading of one of the early maps, as shown on John Evan's 1795 map. Further north, our research has shown there to be no further lengths of Offa's Dyke.

We will now go on to consider further evidence from our research that can help to throw light onto the function of Offa's Dyke. Having established the actual limits of the Dyke, we now turn to the question of whether it was a continuous, unbroken earthwork or whether there were passageways through it at intervals. The resolution of this question would shed considerable light onto how the Dyke was intended to function and possibly even for how long.

Marking out features (27)

In several excavations a small bank, with or without a shallow ditch, or a substantial post have been observed under the bank. Taken together, these features would seem to indicate that a system of marking the course the earthwork was to follow was undertaken prior to its being built. The evidence further suggests that this was carried out no more than a year in advance as there is little or no evidence for either silting of the shallow ditch or of vegetation

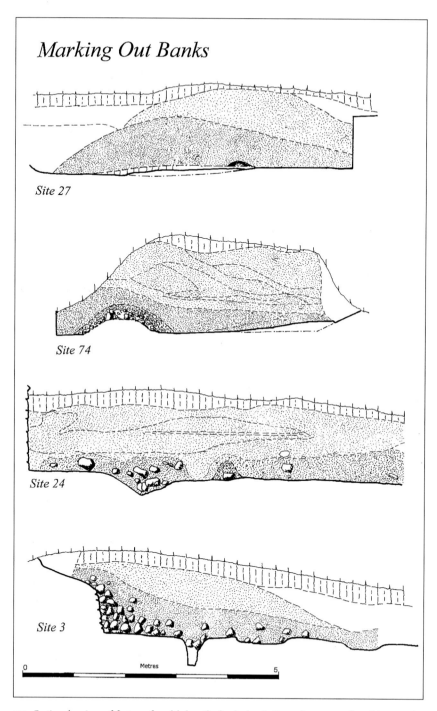

Marking Out Banks

Site 27

Site 74

Site 24

Site 3

0   Metres   5

27 *Section drawings of features found below the bank that indicate the system of marking out the line before the Dyke was built (see chapter 5)*

growing on the small bank prior to the main bank being built. That only a small number of sites have shown this feature is not surprising as only where the bank was built over them would they be preserved. If the ditch rather than the bank had been dug where the line was indicated, then clearly all trace of such a feature would be lost. The number may be small but it is significant and a suggestion of how the line was laid out in advance is discussed in chapter 5.

Gateways (28)

Over the years, the question of gateways has been investigated. If the Dyke was built with a large number of passageways it could be seen as indicating that the builders expected people to be able to gain access but that the access might be controlled or stopped altogether if necessary. A small number of passageways though might indicate a closer control of traffic between Mercia and Powys. If, however, there were no passageways in the original construction it would present a very different view of how the Dyke was intended to function, for then it would be a continuous barrier with no access for either side. Cyril Fox favoured a small number of entrances and suggested several that, from the surface evidence, appeared to him to be original. Frank Noble postulated a model that required frequent passageways for the purposes of agriculture. This was because he saw the Dyke as being set back from the actual boundary with Powys and so cutting across Mercian agricultural holdings. Neither Fox nor Noble tested their hypotheses by excavation. It would have been sterile to have simply produced yet another theory and so a programme of excavation has been undertaken over a number of years.

Our premise, based on other Anglo-Saxon defensive structures, has been that it is unlikely that the construction would have included complex gateways and bridges. A simple causeway, similar to those found at the gates to later Anglo-Saxon towns, is considered to be the most likely form that any passageway would take. It was normal practice in the Anglo-Saxon period, and indeed earlier, to leave a causeway at an entrance through a defensive structure

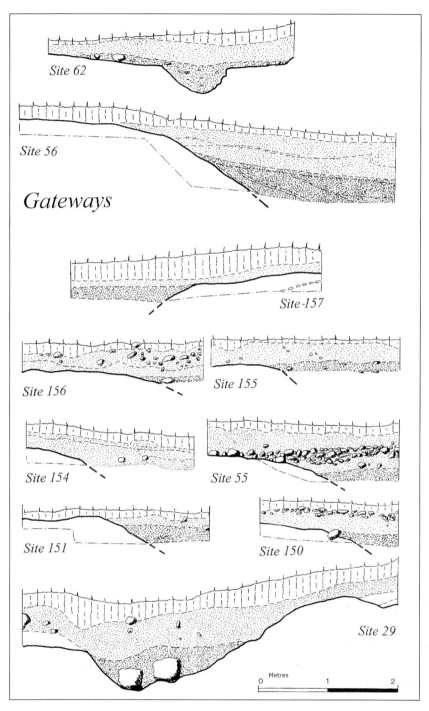

28 *Section drawings of postulated gateway sites; the lip of the ditch can clearly be seen, indicating that the earthwork was originally continuous at these points and therefore they were not gateways through the Dyke*

rather than digging a continuous ditch that necessitated the construction of a bridge. The ditch would simply not have been excavated where any gateway was needed. It follows from this that any excavation that discovers the evidence for the ditch shows that a gateway had not been part of the original design at that point and therefore it is unlikely that any present gap in the bank was an original feature.

Initially the sites suggested by Fox to be original openings through the Dyke were investigated at sites 29 Orseddwyn, 55 Rownal Covert, 56 Kerry Ridgeway and 62 Newcastle Hill. The other two sites favoured by Fox were at Hope on Long Mountain and Frydd Hill near Knighton. The site at Hope near Buttington has not been examined and further research in the area is discussed below. The Ffrydd Hill site shows clear surface evidence for bank and ditch and it is unclear why Fox was so interested in the possibility of a gateway here. In all other cases, the excavation found the infilled ditch below the modern ground surface, suggesting that no gateway had existed at these points.

Houghton's excavations on the Kerry Ridgeway (site 20, above) are of interest for this problem. In the most westerly trench a surface of post-Roman metalling was found overlying the eroded base of the bank of the proposed Roman road (*agger*), in the central trench the eroded *agger* was again found but here the post-Roman metalling was to its south – that is closer to the present-day road. The most easterly trench, still some 50ft to the west of the bank of Offa's Dyke, found the *agger* with the post-Roman road still further to its south with the possibility that it extended some short distance below the present road surface. The conclusions reached by Houghton, coloured by the work of Fox, suggested that the Roman road had fallen out of use when the Dyke was constructed and that the Dyke was deliberately built across the line of the Roman road to compel travellers to turn southwards through the narrow gateway that Fox had identified as a possible original opening. However, this site (56, Kerry Ridgeway) was one of the ones we investigated and found evidence for the ditch. This was not therefore an original opening and Houghton's theory was not proven. It has not been possible to examine under the tarmac surface of the road that now runs along the Kerry Ridgeway at this point and it is possible that the Roman road did follow the ancient way here as they did elsewhere. If this were true then it would be an ideal place to investigate further but archaeological trenches across modern roads, however little traffic they carry, are not easy to arrange.

These investigations were producing negative results but did not prove the hypothesis. It was decided therefore to concentrate on a limited length of Dyke and to examine all the entrances that appeared on a first edition 1:25000 Ordnance Survey map. Any that appeared after this would of course be modern cuts through the earthwork. The area chosen was the lowland length through the Vale of Montgomery where the proximity of crossing places over the River Severn has produced a number of postulated trackways from earlier times. It seemed likely therefore that this ancient landscape with good agricultural land would be a likely place for gateways. The length to be tested was from the River Camlad in the north to the River Caebitra in the south, a distance of some 6km. This included the gap at Rownal Covert that Fox had suggested was original and would also address Noble's hypothesis of many entrances in an agricultural landscape. The monument along this length is in an excellent state of preservation, allowing a detailed examination of all the potential gateways identified from the maps. Eight gaps were found along a 4km length with only one modern road, between Montgomery and Chirbury, cutting the monument. A metalled driveway cuts the Dyke in Lymore Park and it was not possible to examine this break, but the rise and fall of the metalled surface as it crosses the line of the Dyke would suggest that the monument had been levelled to provide access.

Permission was sought from both Cadw and English Heritage to excavate within the protected area of the monument which here forms the modern boundary between England and Wales. To minimise disturbance of the Dyke it was agreed that each trench would be limited in width and would only be excavated to a level that gave a clear indication of the presence or otherwise of a filled-in ditch but that the deep ditch deposits would not be disturbed.

The most southerly site investigated as part of this intensive search for evidence of gateways (site 157, Lower Gwarthlow, SO 243 954) was at a point where the bank and ditch to the south of the modern gateway were in good condition with the western field boundary on the outer lip of the ditch and forming the modern boundary between England and Wales. To the north, the modern national boundary changes to the line of the bank and the field boundary does likewise. Here we find a reduced bank and an apparently infilled ditch with only a hint of its former width at the surface. The excavation in the gateway was positioned in line with and close to the point where the open ditch to the south ended. A great deal of hard core was found in the upper layers and it was clear that this entrance has been much used in modern times. However, the eastern side of the ditch was located and it would seem that Offa's Dyke was continuous at this point in the past.

The excavation, site 153, Chirbury Road (SO 235 974) was adjacent to the Montgomery to Chirbury road. It was clear from surface evidence that the earlier line of the road had passed through the gap in the Dyke as it could be traced to east and west of the gap. The present road represented a straightening of the old road. The excavation encountered a considerable thickness of well-laid cobbles overlying a layer of smaller stone. Below this the western face of the ditch could be seen cut into the natural strong clays with silting within the ditch. The thickness of stone of the old road was greatest across the ditch, as one would expect. A similar situation was encountered at site 156, Dudston Covert (SO 237 967).

At site 154, Chirbury (SO 235 972) a narrow gap in the bank was examined despite there being slight evidence for an infilled ditch. The area appeared to have been disturbed and it eventually became clear that a full-scale ditch had been excavated at the time the monument was built, but that at some later date the western side was filled, the old ground surface still being visible. It is possible that a counterscarp bank had provided the material for this infilling as surface evidence suggests such a feature on the western lip of the ditch a little to the south. There was no evidence of hard core that would suggest that the gap had been used by wheeled vehicles and it seems that it may have been for ease of access by animals from the fields to either side of the bank and ditch, which elsewhere remain in excellent condition along this length. The excavation at site 155, Chirbury South (SO 236 972) found a similarly narrow gap, but in this case the full-size ditch had been infilled with material that appeared to derive from the levelling of the bank. Again no evidence was found of hard core although there is a gateway at this point at present.

Site 152, Rownal Covert (SO 233 979) was excavated for the sake of completeness although it had been investigated earlier (site 55). This was one of Fox's suggestions for an original gateway and some trouble had been taken to carry out a topographical survey as well as resistivity at this point. As the track led into a small wooded area, the traffic through it was lighter than that at the two previous excavations. It was also noted that there was a rise in the ground across the path to the east of the ditch and adjacent to the two ends of the bank that stands to a good height to either side. The surface evidence seemed to suggest a bank, but only the ditch could confirm the continuity of the Dyke. The ditch was indeed present.

Site 151, Calves Ground (SO 233 980) was in a gateway in a position designed to recover the western lip of the ditch. At the deepest level of the excavation an almost stone free, fine silty ditch fill was found. This was overlain by a layer of small stones that appeared to have been put into place when the modern opening was made, but this had quickly rutted and larger stones filled the ruts. A layer of soil and stone had then developed before water-rolled pebbles were laid, with a greater depth at the softer eastern end over the ditch. Thus the trackway post-dated the building of the Dyke and the ditch was part of the original plan.

Site 150, Rownal Paddock (SO 232 984) has a gap in the bank which was examined at the lowest point in a field where the earthwork is substantial and unbroken to north and south within the field. The evidence for the ditch exists in some parts of the field but neither bank nor ditch could be detected on the surface at this point. The ground surface in the hollow was dry at the time of the excavation although it was clear from the amount of hard core that had been laid that this was normally a very wet area. A trench was excavated to the east side of the hedge, here on the approximate line of the ditch but any clear evidence for a ditch was impeded by a working field drain lying along the boundary, a not uncommon feature in the infilled ditch. It was felt that there was some evidence for the eastern lip of the ditch but the evidence was not conclusive, so a second trench was opened on the west side of the hedge to try to locate the western lip of the ditch. Again there was some evidence for softer ground where the trench lay across the extrapolated line of the ditch but certainty proved impossible because of the depth of animal disturbance in the frequently waterlogged ground.

All the openings investigated were found to have had a ditch in place below ground and therefore presumably a bank also. Two of the eight excavations also had cobbled trackways over the infilled ditch representing medieval routes between Montgomery and outlying areas.

There are of course modern roads crossing the Dyke in the area which are difficult to investigate but a major road through the Dyke was tested opportunistically, by Shropshire County Council, during roadworks and the ditch could be seen in the section of their trench (site III, Blue Bell, p.60).

From the evidence recovered in these excavations, it clearly cannot be considered proven that Offa's Dyke was built without any entrances through it. However, when taken with the results of the investigations of those 'gateways' suggested by Fox and by the evidence for the ditch found by Shropshire Highways in the road adjacent to the Blue Bell (site III), it does seem a distinct possibility. If there were no gateways, or if they were very few and far between, it was a situation that could not have lasted for long given the interconnectivity of the local populations. Perhaps we should think in terms of a Berlin Wall; erected to meet a particular need at a particular time and totally unnecessary when the political situation changed. Alternatively, of course, we might have been working to the wrong hypothesis and, unlike any other known example of Anglo-Saxon defensive work, Offa's Dyke had complex bridges. This does not seem likely on the present evidence.

In a further attempt to shed light on this problem, excavations were undertaken on a suggested Roman road on Long Mountain to the north of the Vale of Montgomery. This was a line suggested by Mr Rigg, a former archaeological surveyor in the area for the Royal Commission, who had also spent considerable time after retirement investigating a network of possible Roman routes that he had identified. His work has not been generally accepted, but his undoubted experience in the area and his eye for landscape suggested that it would be worth further investigation when the possible Roman road was brought to the attention of the author (Margaret Worthington) by members of the Shropshire Archaeological Society.

The suggestion was that there was an upland route along the spine of the Long Mountain that provided a dry routeway when the valley route was too waterlogged, a common occurrence in the area. This route was running to the Roman fort and ford on the River Severn at Forden and from there to the fort at Caersws. Mr Rigg felt that a direct route from Long Mountain to Welshpool and from there into upland Wales would be likely, otherwise it was necessary to travel to Caersws and double back to gain access to the uplands beyond Welshpool. A route for this possible branch road had been suggested in his work and it was clear that, if such a Roman route could be proved, it would have implications for Offa's Dyke and the possible entrance at Hope. Fox had suggested an original gateway here and, although this does not look likely on surface evidence, any Roman route might have continued as a track into Offa's time and would therefore be an excellent candidate for investigation. First, however, the presence of such a route, its date and the point at which the Dyke intersected it, had to be established.

Two excavations have been carried out across the proposed route some distance up the hill from Offa's Dyke, as it was necessary to look at an undisturbed section to gain evidence of date and purpose. The first excavation was difficult to interpret as the ground had been levelled in the past by the present landowner. There was some indication of a surface of stone set in stiff clay and with one definite ditch adjacent to it within the excavation. There was, however, no dating evidence and there was a possibility that it represented a former field boundary ditch. The feature we had excavated was adjacent to the present road but the line of this was not finalised until the mid-nineteenth century as the land had been held in common and the steep gradient of the hill prevented wheeled vehicles from being used until they became motorised.

In a second season of excavation a trench was laid out across a feature in a field lower down the slope. This feature appeared at the surface and provided a reasonably good geophysical and topographical plot that suggested a linear feature consisting of a flat area between two ditches; a classic form for a Roman road. This time the feature was a good distance from the modern field boundary to its north and was not on the line of an old boundary that was known to have crossed the field to the south in the past. Thus, we seemed to have a feature that had no connection with any field boundaries or the present road. On investigation, the feature proved to be very similar to that found in the previous season but here the excavation was wide enough to locate a ditch to either side of the clay-with-stone surface. The surface here was less disturbed and gave a clearer impression of being deliberately laid. As with the earlier excavation, no finds could be dated to before the seventeenth century. However, several archaeologists working in the district came to see our progress and all agreed that it was a typical form for a Roman road and could not think of another period when such a structure would be appropriate but could not of course declare it to be Roman without good dating evidence. Mr Rigg had no such doubts and he may well be correct.

The two fieldworkers who originally brought the possibility to the author's attention continue to try to trace the line down to Offa's Dyke but so far without success, or rather with too much success as four possible continuations have been identified. There is the possibility that we are looking at a medieval track that was unfenced and so changed course over the years, or diverted to various buildings long since lost to us. Without more positive evidence of route and date the potential for shedding light onto the original form of Offa's Dyke remains a remote possibility.

Our programme of excavations designed to identify early gateways through Offa's Dyke has shown them to be either non-existent or extremely scarce. Now Roman fortifications have wide and frequent gates that allow a fort to be used as a secure base for counter attacks. If our evidence concerning the paucity of gates on Offa's Dyke is a true reflection of the whole of the earthwork, then it must reveal something of the tactical use of the earthwork.

River crossings

The question of surface water has also been subject to investigation. It is clear on the ground today that there are places where the Dyke presents a significant barrier to drainage. Our survey has shown that, where possible, headwaters of small streams are avoided to minimise this problem. However, for most of its length the Dyke is built on the western slope of hills slightly down from the crest and in this position it does cause problems today. Indeed many of the modern gaps seem to have been cut to relieve this problem. It is possible that culverts were incorporated into the design taking water through the bank and draining into the ditch. None have so far been found. It is also possible that brushwood was laid as a culvert instead of a stone-built one and these would be extremely difficult to find. Two excavations were specifically sited to investigate this possibility (sites 128, Nutwood north and south) but no evidence was found.

In addition to small streams and surface water drainage, there are a number of larger streams and rivers that are crossed by the Dyke. The surface evidence adjacent to many of the small streams suggests that the Dyke was built right up to the banks as it still stands today with no evidence that the stream has changed its course in the interim. Larger rivers, particularly where they flow over a floodplain, are more difficult to investigate as the power of the river is likely to have washed away the bank and infilled the ditch in several places as the meandering river changed its course. An investigation was carried out adjacent to a major river, the Camlad, at sites 117 and 118 where the ditch was found close to the riverbank, and evidence within the bank suggests it was also evident in the present riverbanks. Whilst this is suggestive, it does not prove the case as the Dyke is not upstanding here across a fairly wide area of the floodplain. The likely situation, however, is that it did indeed run up to the eighth-century banks of the river and that the river, more a route than a barrier, was blocked by stakes to prevent boats from using it.

The situation on the River Severn between Buttington and Llandrinio is more difficult to resolve and investigations here are ongoing as has been described above.

Fortifications

Any evidence for watchtowers or more substantial forts attached to Offa's Dyke would give a clear indication of how it functioned and would be the most likely places in which to find artefactual evidence that could also give us a physical date for the monument. Despite our extensive fieldwork and examination of aerial photographs, no such fortifications have been found. A different possibility, and one that fits with what is known about fortifications in Anglo-Saxon England, may have been the reality in Offa's day. It may be that, instead of manned forts attached to the Dyke itself, there were a series of defended settlements set a few kilometres back from the Dyke that were used as hosting places in times of trouble. Thus when the alarm was raised, or when a known attack was threatened, all those who were liable to service in the defensive force would know to which settlement they should report.

There are a number of settlements a short distance to the east of Offa's Dyke that have Anglo-Saxon place-names that suggest a fortification, although it has to be admitted that these are common in many other areas. The significant names have the ending '-bury' signifying a possible fortification, for example Maesbury and Chirbury, or '-wardine' meaning an enclosed place, for example Leintwardine. These places could be used to store equipment and food supplies as well as acting as rallying points. A number of those closest to the Dyke were the caput for their hundred at Domesday, suggesting an administrative importance, at least at a later date. This is of course pure speculation, but, if true, it would fit with the probability that men on horseback were the most likely way that the Dyke was patrolled in times of trouble. A continuously manned frontier in the Roman style does not fit with the known evidence of Anglo-Saxon methods of raising an army or of defensive sites.

There is also the likelihood that a system of beacons was in place to raise an alarm. Such beacon sites are known elsewhere in Anglo-Saxon England but to date none have been found along Offa's Dyke. It should be noted that our very good friend, Tony Clark, was interested in the question of where the builders of the dykes were living. He envisaged campsites with very little structure, possibly near a spring. This theory was based on his work on the Wansdyke. However, neither campsites nor beacon sites were ever located on Offa's Dyke although samples were taken from various promising areas along its course.

The date

Various attempts have been made to find a way of dating Offa's Dyke that was independent of the traditions of its name and Bishop Asser's statement. During the nineteenth century, with the rise of antiquarianism in Wales and the attendant interest in archaeology, some discussion of the Dyke began. The idea of investigating the Dyke at its intersection with known Roman roads did not in fact lend itself to a clear-cut answer.

A different line of attack became clear in 1828 with the discovery of a Roman altar during the levelling of Offa's Dyke at Ffrith, Clwyd. In about 1870, men who were digging the foundations of a new house found flue and other tiles together with a concrete floor in the same area. In 1875, the remains of walls that were strongly cemented with hard mortar were also found, this time associated with Samian ware giving a clear Roman date. All this evidence was found in undisturbed ground making it evident that the Dyke had been thrown up over the site of a Roman dwelling.

Thus, a post-Roman date seemed unchallengeable until Professor McKenny Hughes arrived in Ffrith in 1892 with his theory that the Dyke was pre-Roman and the work of the local Iron Age tribe, the Ordovices. The earlier work at Ffrith, therefore, did not fit with his theory so he carried out some confused excavations at Ffrith, not on the line of the Dyke but in a back garden (site 70).

Cyril Fox's work also attempted to confirm a post-Roman date in several places, including Ffrith (sites 3 and 4); Bryn Hafod, Forden (site 6) and The Steps, Mansell Gamage (site 7). Only at Ffrith was he successful. Thus we have clear evidence of a post-Roman date, but still lack any modern scientific dating as there has been a lack of any artefacts from the excavations and no material that would allow either radiocarbon or dendrochronological dating. This is where the matter has rested except perhaps for some recent suggestions in the popular media that Offa's Dyke is Roman in date, a dating that would have to ignore the excavated evidence at Ffrith. The ideas arise from two facts: firstly, there has been a single radiocarbon date for material found on Wat's Dyke that suggests that this earthwork could be as early as late-Roman or sub-Roman; secondly, an inability of the authors of these suggestions to differentiate between Wat's Dyke and Offa's Dyke which are two completely separate earthworks. There is no scientific dating but there is little reason to dispute the excavated evidence, Asser's statement or the place-name tradition. Thus, the suggestion of a date during Offa's reign (AD 757-795), probably towards the earlier part of it as this was when King Eliseg of Powys was successfully fighting the Mercians along his border.

The monument

Thus the evidence for this earthwork in the central Welsh Marches – that is the length that has traditionally been called Offa's Dyke – shows that it consists of a bank, now much eroded in places, and a ditch on the western side. An outer or counterscarp bank on the western side may have been a much more general feature than now survives, or it may simply have been built in areas of special need such as steep slopes. The scale of the surviving structure in places is 'monumental', in others it has to be searched for with diligence, and it might be thought that this was related to the original planned scale in various sections. However, excavations have shown that the ditch, with few exceptions, is 2m deep and 7m wide and it is reasonable to expect that the bank would have been a mirror image of this, giving a bank at least 2m high and 7m wide and in fact the bank still stands to more than 3m high in places. Our detailed survey of a number of lengths of the monument has also shown that there is a consistent relationship between bank and ditch in that the distance between the crest of the bank and the centre of the ditch is approximately 7m except on the steepest slopes. Excavation has shown evidence of turfs in a number of places, sometimes appearing to form a stabilising front to the steeper, western side of the bank as it drops directly into the ditch. Evidence for marking out banks and posts has been found under the bank in some of our excavations and these seem to locate the line prior to the actual builders arriving to do the work. There appear to be no gateways through the original monument. This is a carefully laid out and constructed monument that appears to have a single plan although its exact form varies in relation to the local topography. Any sinuosity in the line is not because it was threading its way through a tree-covered landscape as suggested by Fox, but is a carefully engineered defensive line that dominates the land to the west. The line will avoid marshy areas, go round the heads of small streams – but only if it does not have to deviate far from its direct line. This is a well thought out and planned structure that was not a panic response to a short-lived emergency.

Our early excavations gave us the line and filled in some of the gaps. Further excavations were designed to test the possibility of a gateway or a crossing point having been incorporated into the original design at a particular site. The way in which the earthwork dealt with surface water, minor streams and major rivers was considered. After careful consideration of the 82 excavations we know to have taken place on Offa's Dyke (appendix 3), 52 by Offa's Dyke Project and 30 by other organisations, some answers are clear whilst others remain obscure and perhaps unanswerable given the present condition of the monument.

We will now go on to consider the meaning of all of this new evidence.

4

CONCLUSIONS

We begin this chapter by returning to our earliest source, the authenticity of which was discussed in chapter 2. Asser tells us that:

> *. . . rex nomine Offa, qui vallum magnum inter Britanniam atque Merciam de mari usque ad mare fieri.*

> There was in Mercia in fairly recent times a certain vigorous king called Offa, who terrified all the neighbouring kings and provinces around him, and who had a great dyke built between Wales and Mercia from sea to sea.

Why did Asser write in these words? There are some sources earlier than Asser that make reference to various earthwork defences and, although these authors are at times confused and even contradictory, it has not deterred some modern writers from using them to suggest that they refer to the earthwork known as Offa's Dyke, and to place it in a period before Offa's reign. It is worth pausing here to examine how the uncertainty of the early sources has allowed this red herring to creep into modern discussions.

The Venerable Bede, writing in the early eighth century, described an earthwork in very clear terms. He noted that it is not a wall because a wall is built of stone, but an earthwork is built 'with sods cut from the earth' with a ditch to its front and topped by a palisade of logs. He describes this prior to stating that Severus built such an earthwork from sea to sea and fortified it with towers but he does not identify where this earthwork was built. The Latin version of the Canterbury manuscript of the *Anglo-Saxon Chronicle* uses the information from Bede but adds that this earthwork was 122 miles long. This has caused some modern writers to suggest that we should consider Offa's Dyke to be Roman.

Bede was gathering much of his information on the early history of Britain from the sixth-century British writer, Gildas, who thought that the northern fortifications were only built after the Roman troops had withdrawn from Britain. Gildas certainly would not consider a wall or an earthwork along the line of Offa's Dyke necessary as this area was still firmly British at the time he was writing. The enemies Gildas identified were the Picts and the Scots, neither of whom could have been contained by an earthwork with its ditch set against the British kingdoms in Wales and the west. Bede was aware that Gildas' chronology for the northern fortifications was incorrect and tried to give a better sequence, hence the reference to Severus and therefore the second century AD. Modern scholars usually consider that the references point to the repairs that Severus had made to Hadrian's Wall, although this was then thought to be only 80 miles long. However, modern archaeological research has now shown that this frontier extended along the coasts to east and west, but on a lesser scale, which might suggest that the length given by Bede was in fact accurate, if the wall of Hadrian was intended. The problem with this interpretation of Bede of course is that, living in Northumbria he would have been well aware that much of Hadrian's Wall was built of stone.

The material collected together by Nennius in the late eighth or early ninth century in Wales also includes a 'History' of Britain and one version contains the information about Severus building a 'wall rampart' from 'sea to sea across the width of Britain, that is for 132 miles' and that it was between the British and the Picts and Scots. A different version of the same work contains the additional information that this fortification finished on the estuary of the Clyde. It is unlikely that Nennius, writing from a British viewpoint, towards the end of or just after the reign of Offa, would have confused Offa's Dyke with Hadrian's Wall.

Thus is would seem that Asser, writing close to Offa's time, can be believed when he tells us that it was this king of Mercia who built the Dyke. However, the same early sources that have caused some confusion about the dating of Offa's Dyke have also caused problems about its extent. Asser is following a long tradition of descriptions of fortifications when he states that it ran 'from sea to sea'; a statement that does not fit well with our conclusions that it was in fact built between Treuddyn and the Herefordshire Plain, neither of which can be described as at the sea!

If we trust Asser when he tells us that Offa built the Dyke, should we also trust him when he describes it as running 'from sea to sea'? Our archaeological evidence suggests that we cannot, but we need to look more closely at why Asser might have used this particular phrase before dismissing it. Offa's Dyke is moderately close to the Dee Estuary in the north and the River Wye in Herefordshire but it seems unlikely that Asser would have considered this to be 'from sea to sea'. This convenient Latin tag *de mari usque ad mare* is met frequently in earlier writings than those of Asser. Gildas, in *The Ruin of Britain*, uses it when describing the northern wall built in stone (Hadrian's Wall) that ran straight 'from sea to sea' – *de mari usque ad mare* and Gildas uses it again when describing the woes of the British – '. . . the impious easterners [Anglo-Saxons] spread from sea to sea'. Bede also uses the same Latin phrase when describing the earthen wall he attributes to Severus (*c*.AD 189-206) and a second time, in what is an almost direct quote from Gildas, concerning the stone wall of Hadrian. The *Anglo-Saxon Chronicle*, probably first compiled at the court of Alfred where Asser was a leading scholar, is probably following Bede when, in a Latin version, it too uses the phrase to describe the earthen wall ascribed to Severus. Doubtless the term was also used in other contexts.

It seems likely that Asser, familiar with a range of early Latin sources and writing in Latin, might have adopted this terminology, perhaps without exact knowledge of where Offa's Dyke was, or perhaps he was simply attempting to give an impression of great length. It may be therefore that we should accept this as no more than a literary device, a useful expression, the use of which was already familiar in connection with other great fortifications.

Whatever the confusions in the sources, Bede is quite clear what an earthwork should be. That Offa's Dyke is such an earthwork is beyond doubt as it has the bank made, at least partly, of 'sods cut from the earth' and a ditch to its front, but no traces of a timber palisade or of watch towers have been found as yet. Myers, in his *Ecclesiastical History*, tells us that Offa owned a copy of Bede's *History of the English Church and*

People in Latin. It is unlikely that Offa would have been able to read this himself, but there would have been those around him who could read it or more likely who could read and translate it for him, but we cannot of course know whether this played any part in the grand design for his own Dyke.

Also to the point is the description in the *Royal Frankish Annals* of another major European earthwork, known to us as the *Danevirke*, running across the neck of Jutland near Slesvig. In the entry for AD 808, so nearly contemporary with Offa's reign, it records:

> [Godfrid the Danish King] . . . decided to fortify the border of his kingdom against Saxony with a rampart, so that a protective bulwark would stretch from the eastern sea-inlet, called Ostarsalt, as far as the western sea, along the entire north bank of the River Eider and broken by a single gate through which wagons and horsemen would be able to leave and enter. After dividing the work among the leaders of his troops he returned home.

Now it is relevant to our discussion of the accuracy of Asser to note that this Frankish description of the *Danevirke*, although written close to the time it is describing, is substantially incorrect, firstly in that Godfrid was refortifying a line built two generations earlier, not creating a new fortification, but secondly it is inaccurate in that the *Danevirke* does not run from the Baltic to the North Sea but only across the dry neck of the peninsula from the Schlei Fjord to Holligstedt from whence the River Eider alone forms the frontier. This would seem to offer an informative parallel to Asser's account.

Thus we can reasonably deduce that Asser's statement about the extent of Offa's Dyke does not necessarily conflict with the archaeological evidence.

We must turn now to a consideration of what the archaeological evidence has told us about Offa's Dyke. The exact delineation of the course of Offa's Dyke has been a major interest of the Offa's Dyke Project. This delineation is not simply a conservation matter or a piece of topographical antiquarianism. The line is important in itself as the basis for the interpretation of the intentions of the constructors and should be discussed against the background of the political geography of the time. As we have defined a different line to earlier workers, it follows that there will be an alternative interpretation.

In essence, Offa's Dyke consists of a major earthwork that runs for 103km (64 miles) from Rushock Hill to Treuddyn and is continuous except for the length along the River Severn to the north of Buttington in Montgomeryshire (chapter 3). This definition of Offa's Dyke is based on the archaeological evidence gathered at the same time as our investigation of Wat's Dyke. The same fieldwork techniques were used on both monuments and proved to be extremely effective on Wat's Dyke. When these techniques were used to investigate all the other earthworks that have been suggested to be a part of Offa's Dyke, each length proved to be of a different character or complete in themselves. This evidence is discussed in chapter 6.

The evidence shows that the suggested northern extension of the line of Offa's Dyke to the sea at Prestatyn, now known as the Whitford Dyke, a double-ditched boundary bank, was complete in itself and of a totally different build to Offa's Dyke.

To the south of Rushock Hill, there are only the intermittent and puzzling short lengths of bank and ditch across the Herefordshire Plain to the north bank of the Wye at Mansell Gamage. Again extensive fieldwork has failed to provide even a hint that there was once a continuation of Offa's Dyke here or nearly 60km to the south along the Lower Wye Valley. Fox realised that the severely gapped northern and southern ends of his line presented a problem and attempted to account for the loss of the Dyke in the south, not only the major gap but also the fragmentary nature of the earthworks in the Herefordshire Plain, by suggesting the presence of dense forest, or 'jungle'; and in the north between Treuddyn and Prestatyn, his argument was that it had been too difficult for the Anglo-Saxons to control the area as he considered it to be too remote from their Mercian heartland.

Instead of continuing to look for more Dyke, and the results of our fieldwork suggest that it is not there to be found, or generating arguments for why there are apparent gaps to north and south, we have instead considered the bald fact of Offa's Dyke from the Welsh perspective.

The careful siting of Offa's Dyke in the landscape argues for a military purpose, at least in part. It would be unreasonable to think of it as being thickly garrisoned and no evidence has been found for forts or towers along its length although we cannot rule them out completely. This is not a Roman-style *limes* but it could not be crossed accidentally and any group that did cross it could have been intercepted by the local population before they returned to their homes, perhaps with raided cattle, prisoners or looted goods. Swift guerrilla raids were the preferred Welsh style of attack and one of their aims may have been to destroy crops and settlements as they attempted to regain land taken from them by the Anglo-Saxons, albeit many years before. Thus it is a defensible earthwork rather than a defended one.

Conflict between Anglo-Saxon kingdoms and the various Welsh kingdoms was inclined to break out at regular intervals although they could also be allies. Welsh traditions record the loss of land to the Anglo-Saxons, with the loss of Rhychdir Powys (indicating arable land), in the western part of modern Shropshire being particularly mourned. Then, as now, the actual border between Englishness and Welshness was doubtless somewhat blurred in the borderlands, and inter-marriage normal. This may have helped to preserve the peace for part of the time but, given a strong and ambitious Welsh king in any area, this long-standing wrong could become the focus of armed conflict. Such a king, Eliseg by name, would seem to have been in power in the kingdom of Powys during Offa's reign.

Mercia faced not a unitary or even a loosely confederated state, but a series of principalities and kingdoms; states that could often put their own rivalries well above any perceived need to present a united front to the Anglo-Saxons. In the central area of the border was the kingdom of Powys. There is some documentary evidence for this kingdom in the early medieval period and one piece of physical evidence for the mid-eighth century comes from the Pillar of Eliseg (**29**), a free-standing stone cross shaft at Llantysilio-yn-ial near Valle Crucis Abbey in the Vale of Llangollen that modern scholarship has named for the king of Powys it commemorates (appendix 2, source 2 for full text).

The inscription records that Eliseg 'annexed the inheritance of Powys . . . throughout nine [years?] from the power of the English which he made into a sword-land by fire'. The inscription was transcribed by the antiquarian Edward Llwyd in 1696 before modern

29 *The Pillar of Eliseg in the Vale of Llangollen. The cross from the top is missing and the inscription has weathered but it stands as a monument to the strength of Powys at the time of Offa*

pollution rendered it illegible. The names recorded are consistent with the ruling Cadellin dynasty which may have its origins from before the battle of Chester in around AD 616, as discussed by Professor Wendy Davies, although the earliest sources do not refer to Powys by name. Concenn, whom the inscription tells us had the stone inscribed, is in the genealogies and is recorded as dying in AD 854. As a great-grandson, we might suppose a lapse of perhaps 45 years if all generations were born whilst their fathers were very young or more than 90 years if their fathers were more mature. Thus the height of Eliseg's power is likely to fall within Offa's reign and a date in the 760s is usually suggested. Thus we have evidence that Powys was in conflict with Mercia. It would seem that the time of Eliseg gives us an historical context for a line being drawn along the particular length of the Mercian border that it shared with Powys.

There is also good evidence for the traditional limits of the eastern border of the kingdom of Powys in this period to be, at its widest limits, from Porffordd, in the neighbourhood of Mold, to the River Wye, near Glasbury and Hay (map 7). This would seem to represent a striking correlation with Offa's Dyke as our work has defined it. The boundary defence therefore would seem to be between the kingdom of Powys and that part of the western boundary of Mercia that corresponds to it.

Whilst it is true to say that there is no certainty concerning the exact boundaries of all or any of the early kingdoms of Wales and of Anglo-Saxon England, the available evidence for a Powys/Mercia boundary being defined by Offa's Dyke is striking. It is perhaps the publication of maps that show on one sheet the cluster of Short Dykes, Wat's Dyke and Offa's Dyke, with the many gaps that Fox accepted, that has obscured this simple correlation. If instead we consider a map showing only the proven portions of Offa's Dyke, and without the Short Dykes or Wat's Dyke, the matter does become clearer and the relationship between the central Offa's Dyke and the probable boundary of the kingdom of Powys becomes apparent. Once Offa's Dyke is seen to represent only the frontier between Powys and Mercia, those lengths that appeared to be missing in the north and the south can be explained as being the frontier of Mercia with other, less aggressive, Welsh kingdoms and there was therefore no necessity to construct a barrier. We have been hunting a chimera. The interpretation that the continuous central Marches portion of Offa's Dyke represents the frontier between Powys and Mercia follows the evidence on the ground and has let the argument move from 'explaining away' the gaps to interpreting the evidence.

We must ensure that a Welsh dimension enters into our calculations, and consider that Offa and all the Mercian kings were continually confronting Welsh problems and relations. The Mercians had after all extended their kingdom at the expense of the Welsh. The boundary situation between Mercia and a Welsh kingdom at any given time might be very different from that with another Welsh kingdom at the same time, or with the same kingdom at a different time; much would depend on the individual kings, their strength and their aspirations. This interpretation, which links the pattern of earthwork construction with the eastern frontiers of the kingdoms in Wales, could have a mirror image, as the frontier on the Mercian side may also have been split into a series of kingdoms. We considered in the introduction the possibility that the western part of Mercia during Offa's reign consisted of recently subsumed minor kingdoms or ones that had accepted Offa as their over-king whilst retaining some independence.

If we consider what we know of the boundaries between these Mercian and Welsh kingdoms, we find that the area south of Rushock Hill to the Severn Estuary is occupied by minor kingdoms under Mercian control, an area that is sometimes known as the Archenfield, and there seems to have been detailed arrangements for the peaceful interaction between the Welsh and the Anglo-Saxons in this area. Further south where there is some evidence for an earthwork on the cliffs above the lower Wye Valley, we seem to have a correlation between the boundary of Mercia and the Welsh kingdom of Gwent. In the north, the boundary of Mercia between Treuddyn and the Dee Estuary marches with that of the Welsh kingdom of Gwynedd.

In conclusion, it should be emphasised that the 30 years of effort by Offa's Dyke Project has confirmed that Offa's Dyke runs almost without a break between Treuddyn near Mold in the north to the last major hills above the River Wye near Hereford. All other earthworks that have been added over the years to this earthwork have now been shown to be different constructions or never to have existed except as a line on a map. In fact, all our effort has returned us to the line that the first antiquaries defined, which all the country then knew but which has had to be proved anew for modern scholarship.

So, whether people think of it as Clawdd Offa or Offa's Dyke, the monument is relevant to both Welsh and Anglo-Saxon history for, rather than a peaceful boundary work, it becomes a significant defence for Mercia against pressure from a virile Powys at the opening of the reign of Offa.

5

HOW AND WHY

This section of the book is an attempt to explain, through a series of comic strip sketches, the conclusions and theories so far reached by the authors about the planning, building and functioning of Offa's Dyke. Some are based on topographical and archaeological evidence, others on what is known of Anglo-Saxon methods of raising a force to build fortifications.

We can observe, with the benefit of contemporary sources, that there had been a series of incursions from Wales into the Mercian lowland and we know that Hereford was taken more than once. After Offa's time, successful Welsh raids during the reign of Edward the Confessor, at the end of the Anglo-Saxon period, are charted in great detail in the Domesday Book. Indeed, so successful have the Welsh been over the millennium from 500 to 1500 in holding back advances from England, that the border of Wales only trembled back and forth on the same general line. What the Pillar of Eliseg would seem to show is that Æthelbald, the great king of the Mercians who preceded Offa, had spread his kingdom westwards and had colonised some Welsh lands. Æthelbald was murdered at Seckington near Tamworth in 757 after a reign of 41 years, a remarkable achievement in the Anglo-Saxon period. After a brief civil war, Offa came to the throne and, whilst his reign was long and glorious, its opening was far more parlous.

Offa was faced with the attacks of the Powys Welsh along his frontier, attacks that also included the Welsh permanently reclaiming areas of the border lands and rendering agriculture and settlement impossible in a string of farms and villages within Offa's kingdom. We have evidence of the strength of Powys at this time from the memorial to Eliseg in the Vale of Llangollen (chapter 4). Faced with an unstable frontier where neither farming nor herding was safe, Offa and the

Mercians had to react. This pattern of devastation on the borderlands appears to be confirmed by a small number of pollen samples recovered from under the earthwork that seem to show that cereal cultivation had ceased and open areas, which once had been fields, were covered by shrubs and weeds.

Anglo-Saxon society was organised in a clear hierarchy, the king had a fixed number of aldermen (*ealdormen*) who formed a part of his council (*witan*) and who were responsible for clearly defined geographical areas. There were also sub-kings of outlying areas. These areas were even sub-divided and divided again. So the king would instruct an alderman, who would instruct a sheriff (*shire-reeve*), and he would instruct the hundred courts and so on down to the various estates, villages and farmsteads (**30**).

The major decision taken by the monarch, probably with his *witan*, was to defend the western boundary of their lands with a fixed defence. The choice of the line of this defence and its method of construction was not a simple one. What should be protected? Such a fixed defence was an enormous investment in time and effort and needed to be thought through before work began. Thus the process of building Offa's Dyke began with a three-fold decision, firstly that it was necessary, secondly that it was possible to construct such a great earthwork and thirdly there was the equation of the degree of benefit relative to the effort involved. How much protection could be afforded for how much effort? Clearly the balance was in favour of the building of the earthwork.

The second question then had to be addressed: was it possible? This was a major, a very major, undertaking. Today it would involve many millions of pounds, taxes, assessments, committees and so forth. The evidence that the Dyke was built is clear to see today, although the method by which it was built has led to some dispute amongst scholars. Some early writers suggested that teams of Welsh slaves toiled away for months or years but this theory must be a non-starter influenced by tales of Roman practice, although even there it was the legionaries who did much of the military work. The other consideration must have been that Welsh slaves or prisoners of war would have been only feet away from freedom; with one bound they would have been free! Unlikely! There are also practical considerations such as guarding, feeding and housing such a workforce for a long period that have to

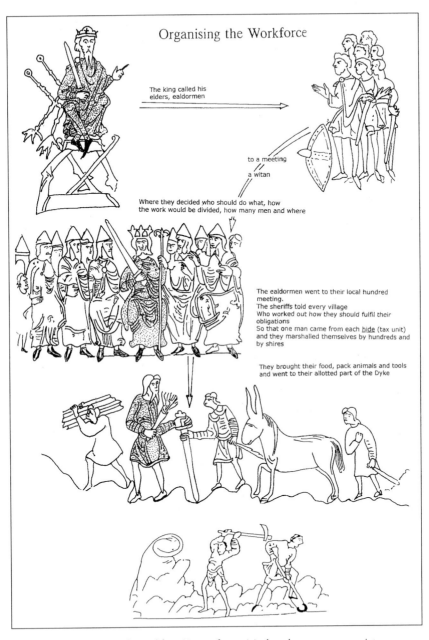

Organising the Workforce

The king called his elders, ealdormen

to a meeting
a witan

Where they decided who should do what, how the work would be divided, how many men and where

The ealdormen went to their local hundred meeting.
The sheriffs told every village
Who worked out how they should fulfil their obligations
So that one man came from each <u>hide</u> (tax unit) and they marshalled themselves by hundreds and by shires

They brought their food, pack animals and tools and went to their allotted part of the Dyke

30 *Organising the workforce. Drawn from original tenth-century manuscripts*

be solved before the theory that slaves were used can be considered to represent a workable system.

The Anglo-Saxons could organise themselves in a most efficient way and once the decision was made to build the Dyke they would have quickly worked out how many men were needed, who should do what, and where they should work.

The calculation of how many men were needed can be deduced from two documents, one dating to before Offa's reign and the other to about 150 years later. The text of the later document is known as the *Burghal Hidage*, because it contained a calculation of how many tax units (hides) were needed to build and maintain a fortification known as a *burh*. It is likely that this or a similar system was already in use in Offa's reign as his charters show that people to whom land was granted owed service for the building and maintaining of roads, bridges and fortifications. The earlier document is known as the *Tribal Hidage* that lists various groups of people including most of the major Anglo-Saxon kingdoms and shows that Mercia was already assessed in hides before Offa's reign.

Using the information from these documents, we can envisage a system where each settlement in Mercia would send five men, as each village seems to have been assessed at five hides and one man was usually required from each hide. These men would be chosen in some way at village level and they may well have seen it as a welcome break from agricultural tasks and a chance to travel away from their village. Documents show that the traditional time for such labour is the period of the year known as the Rogation Days, three weeks after Easter when the grass is growing to provide fodder for the horses and ponies, the weather is usually warm and mild and the days long.

The Mercians and their allies who were called to the Dyke would have brought tools, and those who were not called would have provided some of these (**31**) and a share of the food; perhaps a side of bacon for the men, oats and hay for the animals. On arrival each man, or group from the same district, would have been assigned a length of Dyke to build; perhaps a length per man of 4ft 1½in if calculated in the same way as the *Burghal Hidage*. This document specified that:

> For the maintenance of a circuit of 12 furlongs of wall 1,920
> hides are required. If the circuit is greater, the additional

Spade tip from Southampton

31 *Illustrations of digging and tools from Anglo-Saxon manuscripts*

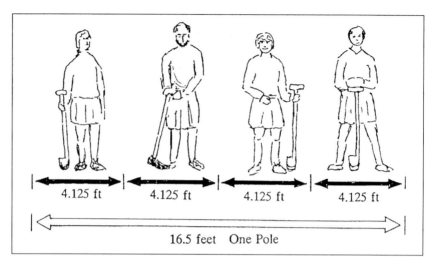

4.125 ft   4.125 ft   4.125 ft   4.125 ft

16.5 feet   One Pole

32 *The length each man had to dig as described in the Anglo-Saxon document known as the* Burghal Hidage

amount can easily be deduced from this account, for 160 men are always required for 1 furlong, then every pole of wall is manned by four men.

So a pole (as in rod, pole or perch) is 16ft 6in, which divided between four men gives us 4ft 1½in (or about 1.26m) (**32**). Working as a team, the men would excavate, collect materials and build their allotted length. They would have worked through all the hours of daylight, as they were accustomed to do when working on the land, and when they had finished they could go home. This was a simple system involving no taxes, no estimates or 'paperwork'.

Now the same system would work the other way, that is from the bottom up. Each village would be known to contain a certain number of tax units, (hides) and usually an average village would hold five hides. The sheriff would know the hidation of his area and the *ealdorman* would know the total of his area of jurisdiction. The total for the kingdom would be common knowledge. Thus it was easy to establish that it was possible to build such a defence.

Once the king and his council had decided what was to be built and that it was possible, there would have had to have been a planning stage, for it is clear from our research that the choice of a line for the

Dyke was not arbitrary. The line taken from one point to another shows an underlying plan designed to cover and protect a series of settlements. However, this desired line was adjusted to accommodate specific features of topography.

Drainage was potentially a problem and, where the land slopes down to the back of the bank, the Dyke would form a barrier that could impede local drainage and leave a stagnant pool embayed on the Mercian side. It is likely that such areas had brushwood culverts inserted below the bank although to date none have been found. We are encouraged to continue our search, however, by the relatively recent discovery of brushwood drains on the much more intensively studied Antonine Wall.

What is clear from our research is that, wherever it did not cause too much additional work, the earthwork was taken to a point above the source of small streams. A greater problem could be the crossing of larger rivers, particularly in the central upland section of the Dyke. It is noticeable in these circumstances that the line taken is carefully chosen to cross the main river below the confluence of tributaries (**33**). This can be seen for example in the valleys of the River Unk and the River Clun. Where this was not possible, as at the River Camlad, River Dee and possibly the River Severn, the Dyke seems to be taken right to the banks of the river and we can only speculate as to what, if any, defence

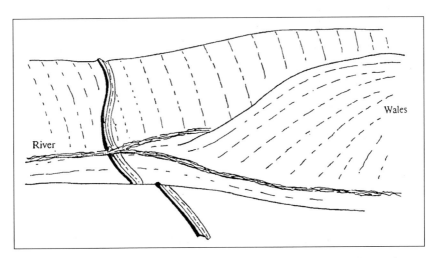

33 *The alignment of the Dyke was carefully chosen to cross valleys below the confluence of two rivers and so minimise the number of river crossings*

was across the watercourse itself. We know that in later centuries chains were set across rivers to prevent Viking boats from travelling further upstream and perhaps a similar arrangement was in place on the small number of major rivers that Offa's Dyke had to cross.

The line taken in the central upland area cuts across the grain of the land, climbing up one steep hillside only to plunge down again into the valley bottom and then up the other side. The crossing of these ridges was also carefully planned as on the Kerry Ridgeway where the line crosses the ridge at the narrowest point.

The complexity of these choices reveals that multiple considerations were built into the overall plan. However, an examination of the more local siting of the Dyke in the landscape shows that the designer or the engineer also had a close control and understanding of the local landscape. Wherever possible the line taken maintains a clear view to the west – that is into Powys. This can be seen in the major alignment across the Vale of Montgomery where an otherwise straight line is sinuous as it passes to the western side of a series of low hillocks before rising at its southern and northern ends to the higher ground (**34**). The line taken to the south of Montgomery is also influenced by the need to take advantage of the westward views along the scarp of the Kerry Ridgeway where Nut Wood stands today. This in turn has to consider the crossing of the valley of the River Unk below the confluence of its side streams. Thus the chosen line always attempts to take a position where there is a clear view to the west, even when this means moving slightly away from the direct line but always with the overall plan in mind.

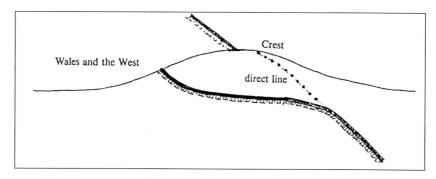

34 *The minor alignments of the Dyke are sensitive to the local topography and curve round the west-facing slopes to keep the view into Powys*

35 *The major alignments may have been set out using beacons*

The line would have been roughly set out using personal local knowledge from generations of Mercians who had lived and campaigned in the area and knew the landmarks. These major alignments would have been set out using beacons or fires to sight from hill to hill (**35**). The more detailed line would then have been marked out with stakes so that minor adjustments to the topography could be made (**36**). Any scrub or woodland would have been cleared, both along the line and across an area either side of it so that it could not provide cover for the Welsh to approach the Dyke unobserved and so ambush the Mercians (**37**). It is likely that a plough was then run along

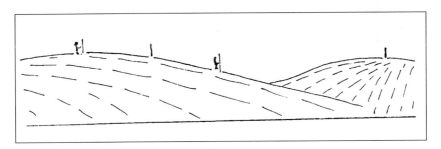

36 *The minor alignments were probably set out using ranging poles*

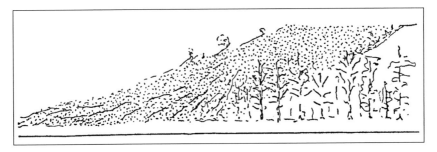

37 *The line would have been cleared by cutting the trees and burning the undergrowth*

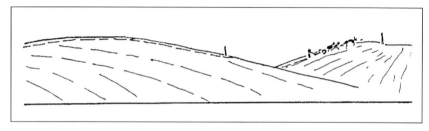

38 Once cleared of undergrowth, the course the Dyke was to follow was marked by a shallow ditch or ploughed furrow in some places (see 27)

39 In other places, the course of the Dyke was marked by a low bank (see 27)

the line to create a furrow to indicate to the construction teams where the Dyke should be built (**38**).

In some areas where it was not possible to use a plough or where the Dyke would not be built until the following year, a low marking out bank of turf or stone, or both, was constructed (**39**), or there was a substantial wooden post.

The excavated evidence shows that the turf was stripped off and used as a material for building or fronting the Dyke (**40**). The ditch was usually cut in one of three formats, a V-shape or a U-shape, each to a depth of about 2m (6ft). The material excavated was used in the construction of the bank together with the turf from the full width of the earthwork. The third type of construction is to be found where the Dyke runs along the side of a steep valley. Here the natural slope was steepened by cutting it back just below the crest and a shallow ditch dug a few metres below the steepened slope. A moderate-sized bank of turf and earth was built at the top of the slope, that is on the normal eastern side and a second smaller counterscarp bank constructed to the west. The whole construction then gave the impression of a considerable obstacle, particularly when approached from downslope (**41**).

In other places the bank has been shown to be too large to have been formed only from the turf and the material taken from the ditch.

Therefore, it would appear to have been constructed mainly of turf from a wider than normal area, or of earth taken from the scoops to the east of the bank that have been observed in some places, particularly on aerial photographs.

The surface evidence for changes in scale of construction can be misleading as the entire earthwork has been subject to different rates of erosion over the centuries. However, excavation can reveal such differences as at Orseddwyn (site 29) where there is a large bank that must consist of imported material as the excavated ditch is too small to have provided the volume of the bank. In other cases, such as at Knighton (site 48), there is a large dumped bank of unsorted material from the ditch and in others a carefully built turf-fronted bank that is stabilised with layers of turf within the main body. These changes of construction along the Dyke leads us to wonder if these are examples of gang work with a group from a particular area using the methods best known to them rather than a completely standardised model. Some of the changes might also relate to topography and geology.

No evidence has been found of the people who built the dyke, neither fieldwork nor aerial photography has found even a construction camp, which would probably be marked by a camp fire or temporary hearth. The idea that the people building the Dyke

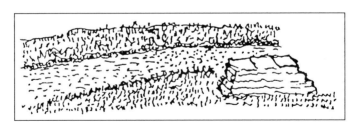

40 *The turf was stripped and stacked to help strengthen the bank*

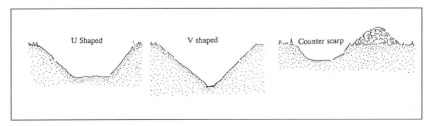

41 *Excavations have shown that three shapes of ditch were dug. The third option, with the counterscarp bank to the west of the ditch, was usually used where the ground sloped steeply down to the west but was also used where, for some reason, the normal ditch could not be dug, as at site 29, Orseddwyn*

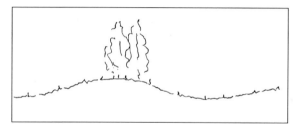

42 *The modern profile, with the bank eroded and the ditch silted, does not reflect the scale of the original earthwork*

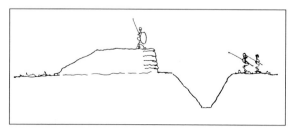

43 *The shape of the earthwork clearly shows that it was built by one group against another, in this case by Mercia against Powys*

camped in specific areas during the construction phase was a project beloved of Tony Clark, one of the pioneers of geophysical survey, who searched diligently along the Wansdyke for such features. Our own searches along Offa's Dyke have also failed to find them, but the scheme for building the Dyke outlined above would make such camps of such short duration as to be almost impossible to locate – assuming they ever existed.

We now come to the difficult question of what it was for. Consider what we have left – a bank of varying sizes and a ditch that can be quite large but is often silted or ploughed over. Much of the evidence for purpose would come from the upper layers of the bank, but this has been eroded away by agricultural use and by the wear and tear of the centuries (**42**). However, we do have some pointers:

> The Dyke dominates and overlooks the land to the west, Wales.
> The ditch and bank always have their steeper face, *against* Wales (**43**).

For many years it was believed that the purpose of the Dyke was to provide an agreed frontier between two different peoples, the Welsh and the Mercians. This is almost certainly disproved by the very shape of the surviving monument that stands so clearly against the Welsh. Where we have known agreed frontiers from various areas and periods of time, such as the Scots Ditch near Carlisle, the Whitford Dyke south of Prestatyn or the County Ditch between Herefordshire and Worcestershire, they are symmetrical and seem to be built by both groups with a ditch on both sides and the earth thrown up in the middle (**44**).

One of the main archaeological problems concerning any understanding of Offa's Dyke relates to whether or not it had a palisade. Evidence for such a structure would come from the original topmost layers of the bank and a policy decision was taken many years ago that we would not add to the destruction of the Dyke and, in particular, we would not damage the finest surviving lengths. Unfortunately it is in precisely these areas, where the crest remains to a considerable height, that the key to the understanding of the function of the Dyke might be found. If, in addition to the asymmetrical form of the bank and the single ditch to the west, evidence could be found for a palisade or a wall fronting a walkway then we might be able to postulate that it was patrolled, at least for some of the time. At Llanfynydd (site 52) and, to a lesser extent, at Orseddwyn (site 29), there is evidence that, once the ditch was no longer maintained,

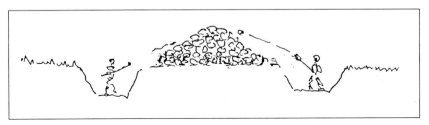

44 *Had this been an 'agreed frontier between peoples' as Fox suggested, it would have looked like this. See the Whitford Dyke in chapter 6 for an example of this type of earthwork*

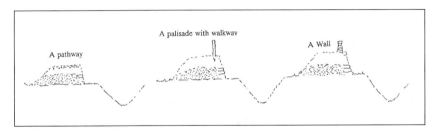

45 *The erosion of the bank has destroyed the evidence for any feature along its crest, but three possible options are suggested here*

the first things to fill it ('the primary silt') were large stones and the implication must be that here at least there had been a wall. We should remember that Offa's near contemporary, Bede, describes an earthwork that, constructed of turfs, was crested by a wooden palisade.

The options for cresting features are: a walkway; a palisade with or without a pathway; a wall with or without a pathway (**45**). Clearly the method of construction outlined above would mean that the workers would each only have to cut a small number of posts to make the palisade, a minor addition to the workload. We have observed in erosion scars on a number of occasions what appears to be stonework near the top of the bank but have felt that this was simply the material from the lowest cut of the ditch that was piled on top of the bank. However, we observed and recorded a large erosion scar recently on Edenhope Hill where the stone seems to have been laid rather than dumped. The line of the field boundary for some distance along this length of the Dyke is to the rear of the bank rather than along its crest and therefore the stone is not the result of an accumulation along the field boundary. It may simply be that the stone was derived from the base of the ditch and was used as a further stabilisation along the crest, but the possibility remains that it was more than this and could have been a part of a defensive superstructure.

Taking the scheme of Earle, of Noble and of our recent work, a guess at the complete working system might look like this. The Dyke has a clear view to the west into Wales with the area directly in front of the ditch cleared of trees and undergrowth. The Dyke forms the patrol line with a path immediately to its rear and our observations suggest that there would need to be a minimum of bridges and fords. A patrol of perhaps ten men moving at four miles an hour would pass any given point at 90-minute intervals, thus there would be a patrol at six-mile intervals, or the 64 miles of the Dyke would need about 100 men at any one time. If there were three shifts to cover the 24 hours then 300 men would be required. The number could be reduced if the patrol were on horseback rather than on foot. It might be that the patrol only operated in times of emergency. All of this is, of course, speculation but without such attempts at an explanation of how it was intended to function, it will remain, in Noble's words, 'a dead monument in an empty landscape'.

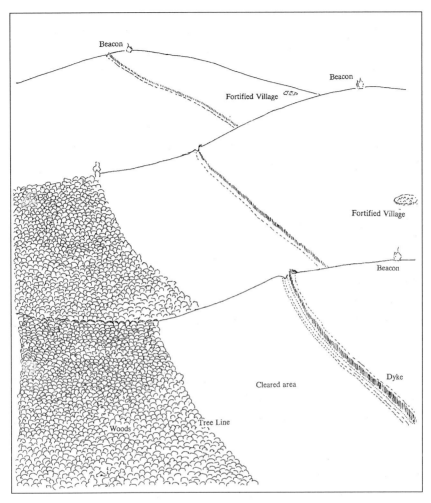

46 *The Dyke did not exist in an empty landscape and the complete system would have involved a cleared area to the west to maintain the views, the fortification of the existing villages to the east to act as centres for the organisation of the local population during times of emergency when the beacons would have been lit*

We do know that the landscape was not empty. A little to the east of the Dyke, there are a succession of settlements with early -ton place-names such as Kington and sites with *burh* (fort) place-names, such as Clunbury, Westbury, Chirbury, Norbury and Lydbury. At least some of these are attested as being earlier than the main recorded *burh* building phase against the Vikings in the tenth century. These places, linked by pre-existing routes, formed a stable line that would have allowed patrols and the general population somewhere to gather in an emergency and to fall back on if the Dyke was overrun. If the line of the Dyke was threatened or breached then the whole patrol system and those living within the *burhs* could be warned by the lighting of beacons (**46**).

Thus we see that the strength of Powys under Eliseg at the beginning of Offa's reign in Mercia gives a reason for why the Dyke was built. A study of Anglo-Saxon documents gives a detailed picture of how Offa could organise the building of the Dyke and our long-term study of the archaeology of the Dyke provides answers to the careful thought that went into the exact line and structure of Offa's great Dyke.

We cannot, however, leave the matter here, as we must also give the evidence for those earthworks that our research has shown are not a part of Offa's Dyke. This is presented in the final chapter.

6

OTHER EARTHWORKS

In chapter 3 we defined Offa's Dyke archaeologically as only existing between Rushock Hill and Treuddyn. We must now turn to a consideration of what the other earthworks are that have been added to a postulated 'Greater Offa's Dyke' and have become embedded in so much modern writing. These suggested additions need to be looked at in some detail and the evidence examined. The area to the south of Rushock Hill will be dealt with in two parts, the Herefordshire Plain and then the Gloucestershire earthworks in the extreme south. The northern area from Treuddyn to the sea will then be considered.

The Herefordshire Plain

In the detailed description so far we have discussed the evidence from south to north. For the Herefordshire Plain the discussion will move from north to south, beginning at the last definite sighting of Offa's Dyke on Rushock Hill (**18**).

It has already been noted that there are a number of earthworks in the Herefordshire Plain between Rushock Hill and the River Wye above Hereford but that they do not form a continuous line, in fact the gaps represent three-quarters of the total length, that is to say, traceable earthworks are almost non-existent. The twentieth-century approach was to find reasons why a continuous earthwork had not been built across the plain. Fox reverted to the explanation of dense forest that he had used in his work on the Cambridgeshire Dykes and in his previous year's survey of Offa's Dyke in Montgomeryshire. Fox's original draft map of the Herefordshire Plain survives on a glass slide in the National Library of Wales and shows the short earthworks in the Herefordshire Plain without any trees, which leaves the drawing looking very sparse indeed. Fox filled in the blank areas between the earthworks by adding trees by hand for the published drawing, as he had to several others. This was to explain why the Dyke had never needed to be built, the forest being so dense as to render it unnecessary. As we have already noted, the belief in primeval forest covering much of Britain at the time the Dyke was built was widely held in the early twentieth century. Our research has shown that in one place described by Fox as the remnants of 'primeval' forest, the tree cover is nineteenth-century landscaping to frame a grand house. The beliefs of the day and lack of time had once more led Fox to a wrong conclusion.

In fact it can be demonstrated that Herefordshire had the smallest amount of forest recorded for any of the Domesday shires along the Welsh border and we know from studies of Anglo-Saxon agriculture that any woodland was an important economic resource and would be kept free of undergrowth by its use for hunting, pannage and management to produce usable timber.

There are many possibilities that might explain the situation on the Herefordshire Plain, the options include:

1 There was a continuous frontier along the Berry Hill and Lyonshall banks and that the gaps are caused (as with the south end of Wat's Dyke) by agricultural practice, this line would then link with the banks to either side of Garnon's Hill.

2 It has been suggested, by Lord Rennell, that the line of Offa's Dyke included the short dyke known as the Grimsditch, the Rowe Ditch and the Scutchditch which lies in a valley known as Sheepwalk, to the east of the end of the upstanding Offa's Dyke on Rushock Hill.

3 Either 1 or 2 above is correct and, as Noble suggested, the gaps were filled by a wooden palisade or an *abattis* of felled trees.

4 The Dyke never went further south than Rushock Hill. The features on the Herefordshire Plain could then be regarded as a disparate and random selection of Short Dykes of various dates, some possibly Anglo-Saxon.

5 The frontier was a series of rivers, such as the Hindwell Brook, the Lugg and the Wye.

When we first began to investigate the Herefordshire Plain, there was a hope, indeed almost a belief, that flying a few aerial photographic runs across north Herefordshire would reveal a simple answer. This evaporated as we flew many times across the gapped areas without adding to our knowledge. This left us with either the hope that, if we waited for the best combination of weather and crop growth, aerial photography might yet provide an answer or, alternatively, we could extend our knowledge by sheer hard work.

Further aerial photography added a little to our knowledge, but the hard work option has resolved some of the problems, though not all of them, and has certainly shed some light onto the options listed opposite. The new evidence is considered below starting from the undisputed upstanding portion of Offa's Dyke on Rushock Hill and working southwards towards the River Wye.

Fox had already attempted to continue Offa's Dyke to the south, beyond its apparent end on Rushock Hill. His suggestion was that the Dyke turned east to run diagonally down the western slope of the Eyewood Valley though Kennel Wood and the Fox map showed traces of the Dyke in the wood as far as the valley bottom in Sheepwalk, although he found no trace here. His suggested line for Offa's Dyke would then proceed across the valley floor of Sheepwalk to join with the short length of the Scutchditch on its eastern side before it was presumed to run down onto the Herefordshire Plain proper. As in Sheepwalk, Fox found no trace of an earthwork in the kilometre and a half between Scutchditch and the next point to the south that he identified as Offa's Dyke.

Fox's suggested line offered the best starting point for our investigations and extensive fieldwork was carried out. The point at which Fox's map showed the Dyke entering the valley at the base of Kennel Wood was located and a trench excavated across the line (site 90, Sheepwalk). The initial attempt to locate evidence for any dyke was abortive, with no trace of a bank or ditch. Further investigations in the dense woodland suggested that the line in the wood on the Fox map might not be accurate as traces of a bank were found a little distance away from his line. The trench was then re-opened and extended and, although there were features in the trench, they did not relate to the normal form of Offa's Dyke in such a location and the features appeared to be erosion gullies of uncertain age. Visual examination and extensive geophysical work in the valley failed to establish any link between the postulated end of Offa's Dyke in Sheepwalk and the Scutchditch or beyond the Scutchditch to the plain.

Some years later, Chris Musson, flying home on a late winter afternoon after photographing the landscape in low sunlight, noticed and photographed a shadow ridge that seemed to indicate that the main line of Offa's Dyke continued directly off Rushock Hill towards the Herefordshire Plain (**47**). He brought these air photographs to our attention and gave us copies. We examined the surface evidence and a possible feature was discernable although this seemed too wide for the remains of the Dyke. One point of note was that, from the end of this feature, the whole of the plain could be seen with Garnon's Hill clearly visible in the distance and, as there are some short lengths of earthwork on Garnon's Hill, it seemed to offer a potentially significant breakthrough.

Two excavations were later carried out, the first (site 140) across the feature to the south of the group of trees known as Box Folly (in the upper centre of the air photograph, **47**). This aimed to examine the nature of the linear feature revealed by the air photograph but the excavation showed that it was in fact related to the solid geology, which here is very close to the surface, and was simply a natural ridge of rock, and so our hopes were dashed. The second site was located to test Fox's suggestion that the Dyke had turned into Kennel Wood (the heavily wooded slope on the right of the air photograph). The upstanding Dyke finished in line with the feature on the air photo-graph but the field boundary turned towards the north and joined the upper boundary of Kennel Wood. A gap in this field boundary, that was not an entrance, was identified and a trench laid out to look for the ditch (site 141). As Fox had suggested that the ditch was on the northern, or 'wrong', side of the bank, here it was necessary for the trench to be long enough to investigate both sides of the bank. The second excavation failed to locate any feature consistent with the ditch of Offa's Dyke. The apparent northern ditch and southern bank described by Fox would seem to be caused by a field boundary of the now deserted Box Folly Farm. A ditch of Offan proportions is clearly

47 *Air photograph showing the southern end of Offa's Dyke on Rushock Hill. The apparent curve to the right into the trees is a field boundary and not a continuation of the Dyke, and the linear feature in the foreground proved to be the result of geology.* Photograph by Chris Musson

visible on the main alignment of Offa's Dyke on Rushock Hill and it would seem therefore that the Dyke does not continue directly down the hill to the Herefordshire Plain, nor, unless it dramatically changes its character, does it continue into the Kennel Wood. In fact it appears to stop on the hillside.

Site 140, Box Folly, Kington Rural (SO 300 595)

The excavation was carried out across the line of the shadow mark on the air photograph that could represent a continuation of Offa's Dyke directly off Rushock Hill to the Herefordshire Plain. The trench revealed the natural bedrock close to the surface, the shadow mark and the visible surface ridge proved to be a product of geology.

Site 141, Rushock Hill, Kington Rural (SO 301 596)
The excavation was carried out to test the suggestion, made by Fox, that Offa's Dyke turned almost 90 degrees from the direct line over Rushock Hill to enter the Sheepwalk through Kennel Wood. The trench was laid out to take in any possible ditch to either side of the slight bank that was visible at this point, but no trace of a ditch was found to either side of what would seem to be a slight bank along a former field boundary.

Site 90, Sheepwalk, Kington Rural (SO 304 596)
A trench was cut in the Sheepwalk to intersect with the line suggested by Fox through Kennel Wood. The trench was extended to cover an alternative line through the wood suggested by our fieldwork within the wood. Although two hollows were found below the surface of Sheepwalk, neither hollow had the characteristics of the ditch of Offa's Dyke in this situation, and their fills suggested that they were natural hollows that had acted as channels for run-off from the valley side.

The continuation of Fox's suggested line was represented by an earthwork that exists to the north of Berry's Wood, Titley, and by an old hedge line to the south of the wood, 2.5km (1.5 miles) to the south of Rushock Hill. On the surface, these earthworks appear to be on a very minor scale, running south from the Titley road towards Berry's Wood, where they appears as a faint earthwork for a length of 126m (138 yards) and this is shown on the 1833 one inch to one mile Ordnance Survey map with a further 126m (138 yards) of more substantial earthwork further south, down the slope towards the wooded knoll of Berry's Wood. Although this slight earthwork had never been investigated archaeologically, it was identified by Fox as a part of Offa's Dyke, appears as such on the Ordnance Survey maps and so is a Scheduled Ancient Monument. Our excavations therefore took place outside the scheduled area where any continuous earthwork would have had to have left evidence of its ditch.

Site 77, Berry's Wood North, Titley (SO 324 588)
A long trench was excavated across a line representing any possible extension northwards of the scheduled earthwork. The only possibility that such an extension would not be within the trench would be an unlikely right-angled turn. There appeared to be nothing within the confines of our trench that pointed to any form of earthwork ever

having been constructed north of the road and it must be concluded that the slight earthwork, visible in the field to the south of the road, terminates within that field.

In a search for a bank or ditch within Berry's Wood itself, neither visual examination nor extensive geophysical work revealed anything of interest. South of the wood, the line suggested by Fox is marked only by a hedgeline and site 78 was excavated at right angles to this extended line of the earthwork, adjacent to the River Arrow and also in line with a short length on the south side of the river, also identified by Fox as Offa's Dyke and also scheduled, although never investigated archaeologically.

Site 78, Berry's Wood South, Titley (SO 325 583)

This trench provided a complex picture of previous river activity but nothing that could be positively identified as a bank or a ditch, although one feature could be interpreted as either the ditch of a dyke that had been scoured out by flooding, or a natural former channel of the River Arrow.

Fox did not believe that the earthwork had ever been built over the knoll in the wood and suggested that it was uncleared 'jungle' from the knoll to the River Arrow, a gap of about 30m and that the built portions controlled trackways, one on each side of the river. However, the built length accepted by Fox on the south side of the river is immediately adjacent to the riverbank.

In the light of our detailed investigations into the Rowe Ditch to the south, and discussed below, we would now suggest that what we are looking at is in fact a cross-valley dyke that is complete in itself and may indeed have protected routeways or have been a land division. These dykes can be of a wide range of dates but the Rowe Ditch can be shown to be early medieval. It should perhaps also be noted here that there are banks associated with old water meadows in the area probably dating to the eighteenth century and the Rowe Ditch had itself been modified in places for this purpose.

Fox's line was continued by the Lyonshall Bank, 2km south of the River Arrow, and the earthworks described near Berry's Wood. The Lyonshall Bank runs for nearly 2.5km (1.5 miles) just to the south of the village of Lyonshall. On the ground it is a broad, low bank with a wide, shallow ditch to its west. It runs from the higher ground on each side of the valley of the Curl Brook. Although only short lengths are upstanding today, Fox marks a much more continuous bank from his observations in 1931 and no doubt agriculture has taken its toll in the interim. This earthwork is again perhaps best compared to the Rowe Ditch, as it appears to be a cross-valley dyke. Excavations have not so far taken place on this earthwork and so its full scale and the question of its termini cannot be determined. In 1994, Herefordshire County Council examined a large area of groundworks and service trenches within an area they considered to be on the expected line, but no evidence of a continuation was found. They suggested that perhaps the line had diverted or been interrupted at this point (site 204, SO 326 563). However, their expectation may have been based on Fox's proposed line to the north of the known bank at Lyonshall where there is the possibility of an extension along the scarp line towards Berry Wood. Fox marks this feature as 'possible frontier', but notes that although the area had been carefully studied, he had been unable to find any trace of Offa's Dyke. In fact, the feature is so close to that caused by agriculture or forestry that until it has been checked archaeologically, nothing useful can be said about it except that the surface evidence is completely unlike that of the main Lyonshall Bank and the name Tramway Pool adjacent to this line may not be insignificant.

In 1980 we flew over the whole area and saw a clearly defined cropmark in a freshly reaped field that seemed to indicate a south-easterly extension of the Lyonshall Bank towards Garnon's Hill. This caused us much excitement after so much negative evidence. However, further research at ground level subsequently revealed that, although this was a genuine cropmark, it was caused by a modern water pipeline and not by an eighth-century earthwork!

Anyone reading Fox's *Offa's Dyke* might be forgiven for thinking that the next length he describes near Ladylift Clump, in Yazor parish, is near to that which he last described, at Lyonshall. However, there is a distance of 7km (nearly 4.5 miles) between the two, with no trace of any earthwork. A suggestion that there might be earthworks on Shoals Bank was checked by fieldwork which revealed nothing but the place-name which is likely to be describing the topography.

As the River Wye to the north-west of Hereford is approached, a length of about 1,085m (1,192 yards) of known bank and ditch can be seen between Ladylift Clump and the northern side of Garnon's Hill.

Antiquarians from the seventeenth century have suggested that the parish boundary over Garnon's Hill was on the line of Offa's Dyke and this has appeared in documents and on maps. If any earthwork here could be proved to exist and be of the same form as Offa's Dyke, it would join the section discussed above with a further section to the south of the hill, discussed below. It has to be said that working in the woods on Garnon's Hill in the 1980s did encourage one to believe in Fox's forest theory as we fought through undergrowth that was almost impenetrable, but the wood was not managed and was not grazed by animals. However, it was here that the 'primeval' forest turned out to be relatively modern landscaping and in the early eighteenth century the hillside had been an open sheep walk.

In exploring the hill, several slight features on the ground could be construed as a built earthwork, although there are also lengths where even this is totally missing. Two small rescue excavations were carried out in the woodland.

Site 73, Garnon's Hill, Bishopstone (SO 403 439)

A feature that was suggestive of a bank and ditch was located but no evidence was found to suggest that this was ever on the scale of Offa's Dyke.

Site 130, Garnon's Hill radio mast, Bishopstone (SO 402 444)

The second excavation on the hillside was undertaken in advance of the building of the radiomast. It was not possible to examine the area where the topography suggested that any ditch associated with Offa's Dyke might have been constructed; this was outside the area to be disturbed by the new structure and could not therefore be investigated. The bank is always more difficult to identify than the ditch, particularly when no surface evidence is present, and, although some differences in soil texture were observed that could have represented the base of a built bank, no conclusive evidence was found.

The intermittent nature of any earthwork across Garnon's Hill might be explained by the fact that prior to the planting of the present wood, the hillside was a sheep walk on which any earthwork could be abraded by the animals or deliberately slighted. The parish boundary crosses the hill and it is possible that earlier field boundaries would have respected this and that these could be responsible for the tantalising fragments found within the wood in modern times. It is also, of course, possible that the parish boundary was drawn along Offa's Dyke but the evidence is no longer apparent. It may be that, should the wood be cleared at any time, a more complete picture could emerge. This certainly proved to be the case in similar circumstances when two sections of Wat's Dyke that we were unable to join through a wood immediately became connected when the wood was felled and a further length of bank was revealed.

To the south of Garnon's Hill, in Mansell Gamage, a further 905m (990 yards) can be seen running down towards the River Wye. Fox's 1927 excavation at Mansell Gamage (site 7, The Steps), was undertaken to recover the line of the Roman road from Kenchester. There were two trenches, one in the orchard to the east and through the bank of the earthwork and one to the west of the earthwork to test the hypothesis that the Roman road had followed a straight course and was overlain by the bank. The published account implies that nothing was found:

> Nothing that could be definitely equated with the road was found; and the complete absence of any traces of the metalling on the *ploughed* field between the Home Farm [to the west where the straight alignment of the road recommences] and enclosure 13 [field west of bank where excavation took place] offered no encouragement to further effort. I now consider it likely that the Roman road crossed the Dyke at the same point as the modern road: by 'The Steps'. If so, its structure here has long ago been worn away by traffic, for the road is in a slight hollow.

However, an examination of Fox's papers revealed a partial report and his notebook for that season contains several references to this trench that make it clear that an article was to have been written by G.H. Jack stating that the Roman road had been found. He notes:

> *Garnons Oct 6 1927*
> Road found 145 feet from centre of road S. of 'W' on 25"
> map. (measured 11 to hedge). It was a thin layer of pebbles,
> irregular surface, with fine gravel in the interstices, 12 inches

below present ground level. 11 feet 6 inches in width. No evidence of ditches on either side but the clayey soil would obscure such if they ever existed. Very irregular surface. Probably most of the road had been 'lifted' by plough.

The excavations were backfilled by 22 October.

It is clear that Fox convinced himself that a road had been found, but on mature reflection obviously came to the conclusion that it did not exist. And that is the view he went on to publish in *Archaeologia Cambrensis* in 1931 and repeated without modification in the 1955 volume that brought together all the annual reports.

A further investigation was carried out by The Steps by Hereford and Worcester County Council in 1992. They were carrying out a watching brief prior to building work within the scheduled area (SO 404 437, site 183) and noted some nineteenth-century terracing and a possible line of a western ditch but no evidence of Anglo-Saxon activity. As this was only a watching brief no investigation of the ditch deposits was made.

The second of the options outlined above included the Grimsditch and the Rowe Ditch in its line and these earthworks have been examined, the latter in great detail. The Grimsditch exists as a place-name and as a short length of earthwork on a map. This could be related to a possible line that ran from Rushock Hill to Garnon's Hill through the Rowe Ditch. A pre-Ordnance Survey map shows what might be a short length of earthwork with the name Grimsditch adjacent to it near Little Sherrington (SO 379 552). The line was easily transferred to a modern map and investigations were made on the ground to each side of the Tippet's Brook using geophysical survey and augering, but we failed to find any evidence for its existence. As the line was so clear from the map evidence, a machine-cut trench was excavated at site 72. The trench was cleaned by hand but revealed no evidence other than undisturbed and continuous layers of stony clay with only one shallow depression that was filled with sandy loam. This feature appeared to be the result of natural processes and had none of the characteristics of being even a field ditch.

In contrast, the Rowe Ditch remains as a substantial earthen bank with some evidence for a western ditch. This earthwork is shown on the Ordnance Survey map to run from just south of the Pembridge to Lyonshall Road (SO 384 578) to the minor road running between Stockley Cross and Milton Cross (SO 379 607) with a considerable gap on the flood plain of the River Arrow. The generally accepted view is that the earthwork had originally extended south as far as Pitfield Farm (SO 383 573) and so at the same time as the Grimsditch was being investigated, similar fieldwork was carried out to the south of this farm to try to establish whether the Rowe Ditch might have formed a link with the former earthwork. The results were negative.

A detailed examination of the Rowe Ditch was carried out over several seasons. A detailed survey was made and ten excavations were carried out across the valley of the River Arrow. These are detailed below from south to north rather than in chronological order, although the site numbers give some indication of the order in which they were excavated.

Site 148, Pitfield Farm, Pembridge (SO 382 575)

Two small excavations were opened by hand to confirm whether the layers identified earlier at site 139 continued south. Clear evidence was found for the lip of the ditch and the upper fills removed. The angle of slope indicated that this was a deep ditch consistent in size with that found on the earthwork to the north.

Site 139, The Plock, Pembridge (SO 382 576)

This excavation showed a 4m-wide ditch that was almost 2m deep towards the western end of the trench. The forward face of the bank was identified at the eastern end of the trench, which would place the main bank under the farm lane at this point. The excavation was carried out by hand during a two-week training excavation in the middle of an very hot and dry summer. The conditions were extremely difficult and, although the results were convincing, it was decided to open site 148 during a wetter season to confirm the finding further south.

Site 137, Football Field, Pembridge (SO 382 577)

The line of the Rowe Ditch had been thought to be along the lane to Pitfield Farm but surface evidence in the football field suggested that the earthwork was further west at this point. This observation was confirmed by the recognition of the eastern lip of the ditch in the field 7m west of the field boundary.

Site 51, The Leen, Pembridge (SO 381 587)

This, the first excavation on the Rowe Ditch, was carried out by hand over an April weekend. The bank was visible but the presence of a ditch was not certain. The eastern lip of a ditch to the west of the bank was found within the trench, but the water table was found to be too high to obtain a full definition of its scale. As the sides of the trench were unstable, the excavation was abandoned on safety grounds.

Site 145, Lane's Cross, Pembridge (SO 380 587)

This excavation was opened by machine at the same time as site 146. There seemed to have been a build-up of water-borne deposits in this area but the upper fills of a 3m-wide ditch were identified. No evidence for the bank remains at this point.

Site 146, River Arrow, Pembridge (SO 380 589)

This excavation was opened by machine at the request of the landowner who wished to improve the drainage of this riverside field. A 1.5m-deep, 3.25m-wide ditch was clearly revealed only a little below the present ground surface. No evidence for the bank remains at this point.

Site 71, Heathy Fields, Staunton on Arrow (SO 379 605)

The bank stands to a considerable height and width in this stretch with some evidence for a western ditch. There is a gap in the earthwork at this point which was investigated over several summer seasons. A long section through the bank and the ditch at the northern side of the gap revealed a considerable V-shaped ditch 5m wide and 2.5m deep. A shallower, U-shaped ditch had been cut into the fills of this ditch in the more recent past. The bank as it appears today is approximately 11m wide with surface evidence of a second, shallow ditch on the eastern side. Excavation showed that the original bank associated with the deep western ditch was 6m wide. The eastern tail of this bank had been modified on more than one occasion. There seemed to be a stone-lined channel centred 4m east of the tail of the original bank and running north/south along the line of the bank. This had been built up on the western side with stone and earth, with a vertical stone face on the western side and a low, rounded bank of stone on the eastern face. The whole had been covered by earth at some stage and over this a different soil had been deposited that filled the gap between the channel and the tail of the original bank and overlay the eastern side of the bank itself. Both of these layers had been cut through and a second shallow channel formed to the east of the original channel and higher than it. This channel gave the surface evidence for the eastern ditch. The whole area then had an upper layer of humic topsoil.

An area within the gap was also excavated and found to have a cobbled surface similar to that found in the stone-lined channel. Fieldwalking found a large area to the north and west of the gap that appeared to have been a shallow pond at one time. To the south a stone-lined, carefully built culvert was found to have been cut through the bank, but the bank at this point had been built over it. Further research confirmed our conclusion that we were looking at a water-meadow system that had allowed a controlled flooding of the grassland to encourage earlier growth in the spring and provide grazing.

The core of the original bank, adjacent to the deep ditch, was shown to have included turf in its make-up. Within this bank a small number of sherds of Roman pottery were found.

Site 79, Vallet Covert, Shobdon (SO 379 610)
There was some evidence in the field to the north of the upstanding monument as marked on the Ordnance Survey map. This was tested and the full-scale ditch, 3.5m wide and 2m deep, was present.

Site 99, Vallet Covert Terminal, Shobdon (SO 379 612)
Further fieldwork to the north of site 79 had found a point at which the ditch appeared to die out and an excavation here exposed the butt end of the ditch and its northern termination on the valley side.

Conclusions

The southern terminus of the Rowe Ditch has not been definitively identified, but evidence has been found for it immediately north of the farmhouse and fieldwork to the south of the farmhouse could not locate it. The terminus therefore would seem to be between these two points, but the farm buildings and yard preclude any further precision. The bank and ditch had been present right up to the River Arrow.

A charter of AD 958 records the boundaries of Staunton on Arrow and these show that the earthwork was already a significant landscape feature. The presence of Roman sherds within the original bank shows that it must have been built during or after the Roman period. Thus, an early medieval date is not only possible but would seem likely. Aerial photographs show considerable Roman remains in the fields around site 71. The Rowe Ditch was cut through these and the Roman material redeposited in the bank.

The important facts therefore concerning the line of Offa's Dyke, are that both a northern and a southern terminus for the Rowe Ditch can be located, and the conclusion therefore is that it is an isolated cross-valley dyke. Thus the possibility of this being a part of Offa's Dyke, or of Offa's Dyke modifying the earthwork, disappears.

There can be no doubt that further work is necessary in the Herefordshire Plain. However, it became clear to us over many seasons of fieldwork that methods that had proved successful in other areas were providing negative results here. Although there are various short lengths of upstanding earthworks, when each was investigated from the air, with geophysical survey, with fieldwalking or with the spade, no continuous earthwork could be discovered and no connection could be made with Offa's Dyke. The bank and ditch adjacent to the River Wye at Garnon's Hill perhaps provides the best possibility of being a portion of Offa's Dyke in terms of siting and character, but so too did the Rowe Ditch before its termini were found. This area, from Rushock Hill to the Wye, has only 5.5km (3.3 miles) of earthworks in the 20km (12.5 miles) of line and most of these have been shown conclusively to be completely separate from, and never a part of, Offa's Dyke. The conclusion must be that, unless further evidence comes to light, Offa's Dyke as a constructed bank and ditch ceased at Rushock Hill. Clearly this does not rule out the possibility that a river system formed the frontier but it is difficult to envisage a proof for this and a palisade would be equally difficult to demonstrate.

The Wye Valley to the sea (48)

This section is unlike the others in this volume in that it is a critique of past workers in our field; in particular it is a critique of the work

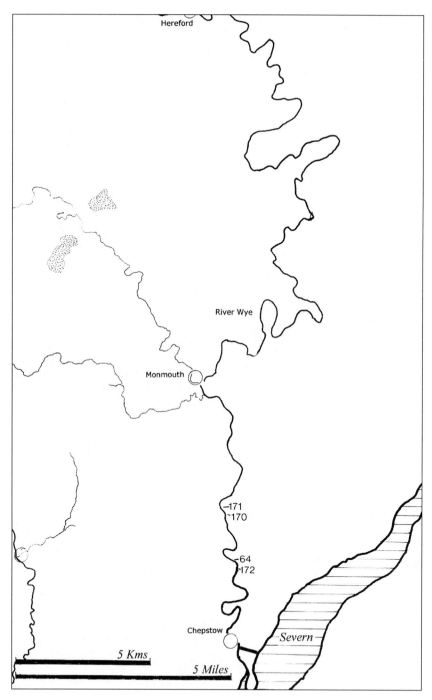

48 *Map from Hereford to the Severn Estuary showing sites excavated across earthworks that have in the past been suggested to be part of Offa's Dyke. See also* **49** *opposite for details of excavations on the earthwork near Chepstow*

of Sir Cyril Fox. This is unfortunate in that, in general, we stand on giant's shoulders, and Fox's work is indispensable to serious studies of the Dykes, in particular as an inventory of the state of the Dykes in the 1920s and 1930s.

Why then is the section on west Gloucestershire in need of serious revision? Primarily because Fox was the 'inventor' of the section. The reasons for this are many. Firstly, Fox was wedded to the concept of Offa's Dyke running from sea to sea, and he was therefore attempting to fill the perceived 'gaps'.

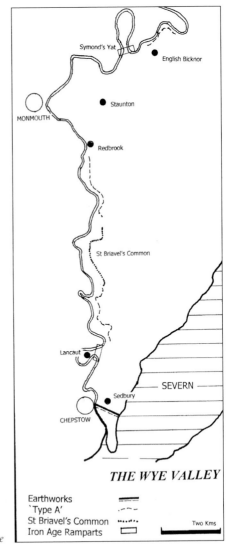

THE WYE VALLEY

Earthworks	
'Type A'	.- ~ -
St Briavel's Common	....•...
Iron Age Ramparts	▭

Two Kms

49 Earthworks described as Offa's Dyke along the Wye Valley can be shown to be of a different structure and, in some cases, a different date from Offa's Dyke. Only the length near Chepstow is of a similar structure

There is a stretch of supposed earthworks along the left bank of the River Wye and it was first suggested in 1840 that Offa's Dyke was to be seen at Sedbury. Now this short stretch of 1.4km (0.875 miles) appears similar to undoubted portions of the Dyke between Treuddyn and Rushock Hill, but even after the suggestion of other earthworks further up the river, it was still questioned in 1911 by Lloyd that these works had anything to do with Offa's Dyke. It was Fox in 1931 who categorically stated that the Dyke was to be found along the Wye. His results were not tested except for his excavation at Tallard's Marsh, which he dated by the 'socket of an iron lancehead . . . though this object is consistent with an Offan date for the earthwork it does not prove it . . .'. Our 1999 excavation discovered that the 'lancehead' was probably amongst frequent finds of fairly recent iron scrap from the site and highly unlikely to be early. Unfortunately Fox's single find is no longer to be found in the National Museum in Cardiff.

Hoyle's review of the evidence for the earthworks in the Wye Valley has removed one class of earthwork: the fortifications from the Iron Age forts of Lancaut and of Symond's Yat. This leaves two classes of works to add to the Sedbury earthwork. One is Hoyle's Type A, some isolated stretches of apparent earthwork on the crest of the river cliffs, associated with quarrying (49). Their date is uncertain and their line discontinuous. There is also the St Briavel's Common earthwork which is a disparate group of features, including a section with an eastern ditch, not on the crest of the slope, but wandering across what had been common land. It is important to remember that Fox was convinced he could recognise 'western frontier-works of Mercia in the seventh and eighth centuries AD'. He also stated that, 'the acceptability of uncharacteristic sectors as veritable portions of the Dyke depends on their being in direct extension of character-istic portions, on an alignment that the Dyke might be expected to take'.

It might not be unfair to suggest that once the fieldworker has decided on the probable line, *any* feature can be pressed into service. Thus a series of intermittent features with very wide gaps was accepted, but we are bound to ask even if these features move in the 'correct' general direction, what evidence is there that they are related one to another, are all of the same date, and can they be assigned to the period of Offa? Only the Sedbury section appears to be possible and this is isolated by many miles from the southern end of the accepted Dyke.

What we find then is an expression of Fox's theories, firstly he calls upon the explanation of forest features to explain gaps; secondly he relates the need for a Dyke, 600ft above the river level, to the tidal features on the Wye, and finally all these disparate features are linked together to the supposed activities of 'Welsh shipmen'. There must be extreme caution before we accept the Dyke, particularly one contemporary with Offa, in the southern Wye Valley. We already know that many of Fox's short dykes are of all periods and only a minority can be Mercian, and we must approach his maps with the knowledge that the presence of so much (impassable) woodland on them depends for evidence on the absence of Dyke features, in other words, when faced with a gap, he drew in trees.

It has been noted above that the Herefordshire Plain and southern end of the Wye Valley to its confluence with the Severn Estuary has 95km (59.5 miles) of line, claimed in the past 80 years as 'Offa's Dyke', but only 22.3km (13.8 miles) of discontinuous earthwork could be recognised. There is a 59.5km (37 mile) gap from near Garnon's Hill, which does contain a fragment, less than a kilometre (about half a mile) that Fox considered to be Offa's Dyke at English Bicknor. The surface evidence does not suggest an earthwork of a similar build to the central portion of Offa's Dyke nor has any evidence been found to connect this isolated bank to any larger earthwork.

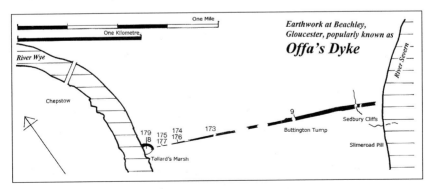

50 *The Beachley Peninsula near Chepstow (see **48**). Details of excavations on this detached earthwork with the enclosure at Tallard's Marsh*

Finally we reach the lower Wye Valley below Monmouth where there is roughly 10 miles (16 km) of intermittent earthwork, which is today designated 'Offa's Dyke' on maps, and terminates at the Severn Estuary at Sedbury Cliff. The lengths on the cliffs above the Wye Valley have been examined in detail by Jon Hoyle of Gloucester County Council Archaeology Service and discussed with the authors. The conclusion seems to be that there are at least three discrete lengths, each different in character and with little similarity to the form or siting of Offa's Dyke in the undisputed central area of the Welsh Marches. It was the acceptance of these lengths as Offa's Dyke by Cyril Fox that placed them firmly on the Ordnance Survey maps, as they had not originally been designated 'Offa's Dyke' but 'Ancient Entrenchments'. That there are short lengths of earthworks on top of these cliffs is beyond doubt, but their date and purpose has yet to be clarified. It seems strange that Fox should consider the River Wye in the lowland reaches below Hereford to be a sufficient barrier but in the lower reaches, where high cliffs protect the eastern side, the addition of what by comparison would be a modest earthwork should be deemed necessary.

The length of earthwork that crosses the Beachley Peninsula in the south and runs between Sedbury Cliffs on the River Severn and the cliffs of the River Wye opposite Chepstow has been investigated in some detail by the Project (50). The measured survey has been completed and seven excavations have taken place, one by Fox in 1930, one by Lewis in 1960 and five by the Project. This section of earthwork is dated to before AD 956 as it appears as '*dic*' in a charter of that date.

The earthwork crosses the peninsula formed by the two rivers from north-west to south-east. It is on rising ground with good views to the south over marshy land. The earthwork stands to a good height, particularly in its south-eastern section, with a ditch to its south. This more southerly part of the earthwork begins on the low clay cliff, known as Sedbury Cliff, overlooking the mudflats of the Severn Estuary that are exposed at low tide. A shallow valley is parallel with and to the south of the earthwork and runs into the estuary through the grass and sea marsh. There is a small stream, glorying in the name of Slime Road Pill, running in the lower part of this valley, but inland it turns to the north-east and becomes a marshy area that extends through the Dyke at the bottom of the slope. This may, however, be a cut for drainage, possibly replacing an earlier culvert. From Sedbury Cliff, the earthwork drops steeply down to cross this little valley, the only gap being for the drainage. As the earthwork reaches the crest on the northern side of the valley, the road between Sedbury and Beachley is seen and the ditch was observed briefly in a pipeline trench that was being cut along the road. The road is situated on a ridge of higher ground between two shallow valleys, one running to the south of the Dyke and ending in Slime Road Pill, the other cutting the line near Pennsylvania Farm. The road leads to the site of the ancient ferry crossing of the River Severn between Beachley and Aust.

Buttington Tump is to be seen on the line of the Dyke on the north side of the road. How ancient the existing remains are is a matter for debate as road widening almost certainly altered its profile in modern times. The Tump was the site of Lewis' 1960 excavations.

Site 9, Buttington Tump, Gloucestershire (ST 547 931)

In the published report of 1963 Lewis records that it was named as Buttington Tump on Greenwood's 1824 map. He dug a section across the Tump with a machine down to the natural subsoil and the exposed face was cleaned down by hand. The section shows a bank no more than 2m high above the subsoil and comprising of mixed clay and gravel at its base with a lens of lime separating this from a layer of yellow sand and gravel on its northern side. Over this was a layer of lime that could have been a later addition or part of the original build. Overlying the whole, but mainly to the north, was a considerable build-up of topsoil. The subsoil below the bank was very hard, compacted gravel. The ditch by contrast was cut into undisturbed red clay. The section drawing suggests that there was a space between the tump and the ditch. The ditch was 3.5m across, its depth is difficult to gauge from the drawing but was certainly in excess of a metre. The Tump would seem to have been a much slighter feature than that seen today. Whether it pre-dated the ditch or was contemporary with it is not clear, nor is its relationship with the running earthwork.

Beyond Buttington Tump the earthwork is somewhat damaged for a short length, but is discernable and again takes a direct line down to the next valley bottom where it is cut first by a disused railway track, but more significantly by the stream, which extends into the ditch here to form a small pond by Pennsylvania Farm. To the north of this point a house had cut into the west side of the bank. The bank to the west of the pond and the house clearly shows on the large scale Ordnance Survey map and this 70m length was included in the list of Scheduled Ancient Monuments in 1993. Since then new houses (Orchard Farm Close) have been built and the bank almost completely destroyed in their back gardens. One owner informed our surveyors that they had been aware that the bottom of their garden was said to be Offa's Dyke, but that the builders had destroyed it. Ponds, paths and greenhouses now cover this 'protected' length.

Beyond these new houses, the older houses on the north side of Mercian Way mark the line of the earthwork. These properties were being renovated during our survey and we were able to record a cut through the bank for a new pipe between numbers six and seven.

Site 173, 6/7 Mercian Way, Sedbury (ST 544 932)

This site consists of an ancient bank on the top of the slope where recent disturbance has covered it with upcast. The natural slope is quite steep and it seems likely that this would have been cut back with a bank on top and a ditch below to give the appearance of an earthwork of more considerable height. It was not possible to examine the whole monument at this point as the present road runs over the presumed line of the ditch.

Beyond Mercian Way, the bank and ditch is visible on the southern edge of the football field adjacent to Offa's Close. The earthwork is overgrown with shrubs and trees and is much used by children for 'dens' and by adults for dumping rubbish. Beyond this point, the line runs along the edge of the allotments and the road. The ground again drops down to a small stream before climbing up again to the cliff edge above the River Wye. Further excavations were carried out in this length.

Site 174, Allotment, Sedbury (ST 542 933)

A section was cut into the roadside verge outside the area of the allotments and opposite the sewage works. The bank, as a steep slope, was visible here as it had been at Mercian Way, but at this point the grass verge to the west was wide enough to allow an investigation of the ditch to take place. An almost complete ditch section was recovered, cut through extremely hard natural deposits at its eastern side at the base of the slope and into strong clay beyond. The overall width of the ditch was 4m and had a minimum depth of 1.5m. A baulk had to be left within the ditch to support a pipe and this rendered a full profile inaccessible, although its general slope to east and west suggested that the bottom of a V-shaped ditch had almost been reached.

While the trench was open, samples were taken by the Research Laboratory for Archaeology and the History of Art at the University of Oxford to attempt to determine the date for the lowest levels of silting in the ditch. However, no date was obtained as the sediments had not been exposed to the sun for long enough after they were deposited for the geological signal to be erased so that a new signal could build up during burial.

The slope above the ditch was also investigated up to the fenceline of the allotments but apart from a thin and recent covering of topsoil, it appeared to be undisturbed and natural. However, the possibility that it had been cut back to make it steeper in the past is not excluded by the evidence obtained. This excavation was continued into the allotments as site 176.

Site 176, Allotment Bank, Sedbury (ST 541 933)

An area was excavated to expose the top of any remaining bank within the allotments and immediately north of site 174. There was evidence of a strip of stiff clay along the hedgeline and to its north. This was within the area normally cultivated as an allotment and survived only as a low feature below the topsoil. It is probable that it did represent the base of a former bank that, because of the steep slope beyond, may never have been very substantial. The soils to the north of this feature were softer loam.

Site 175, Sewage Works, Sedbury (ST 541 934)

A trench was opened next to the lane by Tallard's Marsh Cottage. No evidence was found for bank or ditch and it would seem that the original line was to the south of this point and probably under the lane.

There are no visible signs of the earthwork beyond the stream that borders the western edge of the allotments. What appears to be a 'good' piece of bank just west of a culvert is in fact of very recent construction appearing during our visits to the area. An area of scrubby field is to the east of the road and this appears to have been artificially lowered in the recent past. To the west of the road are the sewage works and then the lane curves round to the driveway of Tallard's Marsh Cottage and footpath access to a part of the banks of the River Wye. On the large-scale Ordnance Survey map an earthwork is marked as an enclosure round the cottage shown by hachures to be a slope to the south becoming a ditch towards the north. The cliff above the River Wye formed the western side. This feature was investigated in 1930 by Cyril Fox and in 1998 by the authors.

Site 8 (Fox) and Site 179 (ODP), Tallard's Marsh, Sedbury (ST 540 934)
The section published by Fox in 1931 shows the remains of the base of a bank of 're-set and dirty' clay over undisturbed clay. The bank material tails away to what Fox describes as a natural depression in the limestone bedrock that the surface evidence showed to extend inwards from the cliff edge. This he believed had been utilised by the builders of the bank – the small V-shaped cut in the base of the depression might in the present authors' opinion be manmade. The top of the depression seems to be more than 20ft across on the scale provided but only 3ft deep into the V-shape; it was filled with silt overlain by material similar to the bank but pushed over into the ditch. A coin of 1806 was found at the interface of these two layers and an iron lancehead on the bedrock below the silt on the inner lip of the V-shape. This was seen as being consistent with an Offan date, but not as proof of the date of the earthwork itself. As Fox remarks, it is of a type known from Roman through to medieval times.

The 1998 excavation was intended to reopen Fox's trench to further investigate the nature of the evidence. Considerable effort was made to locate the trench using the plan published by Fox, but eventually it was established beyond doubt that the published plan and its scale were incorrect. A trench was therefore laid out across the perceived line and at a distance from the cliff that seemed to fit with the ratios that could be worked out between the plan and the actual evidence on the ground. Unfortunately, in the time available and with the lack of good locational evidence, no trace of either Fox's excavation or a depression in the bedrock was found. There was a slight hollow on the surface but this was not found to be mirrored in the bedrock. It would seem that either the depression runs out before our trench or the area has been too much altered by extensions to the buildings, new fences and footpaths to give a false impression of where that part of the earthwork was located.

That the earthwork is so clearly marked on the Ordnance Survey maps and that the line of the linear earthwork across the peninsula seems to connect to it may indicate a common purpose, and possibly a common date. The cliffs at this point are solid rock and high; stronger than those at Sedbury Cliff, but almost immediately to the south there is a shallow valley running into the River Wye. This is the marsh known now as Tallard's but in fact was called Tile Yard Marsh originally. There was a landing point from the River Wye by means of a small tidal inlet or pill that is now silted. This landing is just downslope of the enclosure on the cliff. The ditch of the linear earthwork has been found facing towards the river throughout its length and would seem to indicate an anticipated threat from, or need to control, access from the water. This landing place would be a weak point in such a line and therefore a potential site for a look-out post. Similar points might be at Buttington Tump where the dry ridge route from the ferry crossing point still carries the only modern road to run to the coast and on Sedbury Cliff. All of this is of course pure speculation as we do not even know the period in which either the linear earthwork or the curvilinear earthwork were built, much less the century.

Fox's 1930 excavation report and published section mention the 'iron lancehead'. The position, on the *floor* (authors' emphasis) of the ditch was thought suggestive and the 'lancehead' was seen to be from an early date. Our 1998 excavations recovered several other pieces of, what to us, appeared to be Victorian scrap iron. Thus Fox's find was not unique, its dating suspect and the interpretation of a piece of iron measuring 9mm maximum diameter and 35mm in length as a lancehead unsupportable, although common sense raises the possibility that the published measurements are themselves suspect.

Fox dealt with these enormous gaps in the south in a now familiar way, by reverting to his 'forest' and 'raging torrent' theories. It would be tiresome to rehearse the arguments against 'forest so dense' yet again, although Noble clearly saw this theory's inability to explain the problems and, in one of his most useful detailed sections, considers the whole of this area. He also draws attention to the interrelation of the borders of Gwent to the presence of the earthwork. The rehabilitation of much of the material in the Llandaff Charters by Professor Wendy Davies shows that the distribution of these early land documents does not recognise the forests postulated by Fox, and though the charter bounds mention woods, they are obviously interspersed with considerable (and interconnected) settlements.

The north: from Treuddyn to the coast

In 1703, Edward Llwyd raised the question as to whether there were evidences of Offa's Dyke north of Treuddyn, the apparent northern terminus of the central portion of Offa's Dyke (**25**). Since that date, a strip of country some 35.5km (22 miles) long between Treuddyn and the sea has been intermittently investigated by various fieldworkers and antiquarians.

As with the Herefordshire Plain, several short lengths of earthwork were suggested as being a continuation of Offa's Dyke and our research has been to investigate the earthworks and to attempt to fill the gaps between them by locating evidence for further lengths of earthwork. This situation is further complicated by the presence of Wat's Dyke, a short distance to the east and north, and what appears to be a reasonable continuation of the line north from Llanfynydd that would bring Offa's Dyke onto the line of Wat's Dyke. In fact, many early writers and map makers did just that, starting with John Speed in 1612. The confusion between the two is compounded by a number of minor Offa place-names on the northern end of Wat's Dyke that led to suggestions that this was in fact a part of Offa's Dyke. This possibility was considered by the Project in its early years but, after extensive fieldwork, no connection between the two has been found, Wat's Dyke being complete in itself and of a consistent form.

It was in this strip between Treuddyn and the sea that the archaeological problems of the Dyke were first encountered by the Project, when the canon of accepted earthworks was challenged by the excavated reality. In several places on this hypothetical line there is simply no earthwork. As outlined in chapter 2, Fox believed there was a total of 5.75km (3.75 miles) of built earthwork in this 35.5km

(22 mile) length. Fox was working immediately after the publication of the Royal Commission's *Inventory* for Flintshire which 'identified' as Dyke three portions of earthwork. It identified a trace near Ysceifiog Circle, one near Whitford and another between Tre-abbotbach and Trelawnydd. These and the substantial gaps between have been investigated by the Project over the past 30 years and will be considered from south to north below.

Ysceifiog Circle (SJ 152 753) is 22.75km (14 miles) from the last positive identification of Offa's Dyke at Treuddyn. In fact this site is some distance north of Ysceifiog village but is within Ysceifiog civil parish. The centre is a Bronze Age barrow with traces of a circular earthwork round it and with two short and faint traces of linear earthwork to the north-west and south of the barrow. The barrow is marked 'tumulus' on the 1:25000 Ordnance Survey map and the slight earthworks are marked as 'Offa's Dyke' and 'Offa's Dyke (course of)'. Fox excavated two sections across the earthworks, one 130 yards to the north-west and the other 43 yards to the south-east of the barrow (site 2, Ysceifiog Circle). His published plan shows that the linear sections of earthwork had intersected with the circular earthwork round the barrow but had not crossed it, which suggests to the present authors that the two features were contemporary with the barrow.

An examination of Fox's two drawings of the sides of his trenches, at first sight, suggest that he found the remains of a central bank with a shallow ditch to either side. However, a careful reading of the text and the annotation on the drawing shows that in fact neither an original ground surface below the bank nor the original floors of the ditches were identified. The lines drawn on the sections to mark the ditch profiles are labelled 'original profile of ditch?' and the text states that these were drawn after 'careful scrutiny' and a 'high probability' was expressed that these did represent the true situation. This would give ditches to either side of the bank of approximately 1m deep (3 ft). The bedrock in this area is limestone and the drift geology is stiff clay with stone.

Fox had hoped to establish the original dimensions of Offa's Dyke at this point. His excavations here, and to the north at Brynbella discussed below, took place in 1925, his first season of work on the earthworks in the Welsh Marches. Fox's great strength was his previous experience of linear earthworks in Cambridgeshire

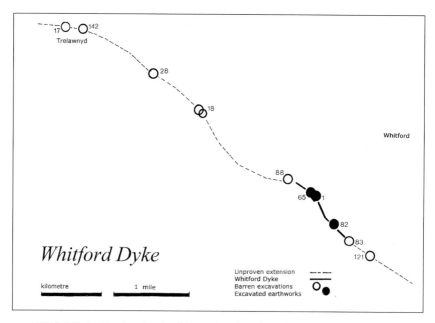

51 *Whitford Dyke. The short length of this earthwork is shown by the solid line and filled circles that indicate excavations with evidence for an earthwork. The open circles are excavations that found no earthwork, those immediately to north and south of Whitford Dyke were exploring any possible extension; those further north were testing Fox's postulated line. See **25** for the location of Whitford Dyke*

and his confidence in his own abilities as a fieldworker. The present authors, with the benefit of hindsight, can only regret that he did not begin his work in the south on the Beachley Peninsula where the earthwork (whether or not built by Offa) would at least have led him to expect a single west-facing, 2m-deep ditch and a considerable bank.

There is today little surface evidence for what appears to have been a Bronze Age complex of barrow and earthwork at Ysceifiog. Several observations in trenches cut for services have been made by the authors and by archaeological contractors across the postulated line of these earthworks and any extension of them to north or south, but no evidence has been found to suggest further bank or ditches.

Some 2km to the north is another 1.5km length of linear earthwork centred on Brynbella Mound (SJ 130 771) (**51**). Excavations were carried out at Brynbella Mound by Fox (site 1, SJ 129 771) after his difficulties at Ysceifiog. At this site he hoped to find a rock subsoil that would make identification of the ditches easier. Two sections were cut, one of which included a part of the mound itself, a much more substantial structure than that at Ysceifiog. The more northern excavation revealed ditches cut into the limestone bedrock to either side of a bank. The second, southerly excavation showed the one ditch adjacent to the eastern side of the mound. The ditches were between 4½ft and 6ft deep (1.3 to 1.9m) although these depths seem to be from the estimated previous ground level rather than the depth observed within the trenches. Fox accepts the bank and ditches as a part of Offa's Dyke and the mound itself as 'sepulchral' and earlier than the linear earthwork. No artefacts were found either in the ditches or in the partial excavation of the mound. This undoubted earthwork is of a completely different profile to Offa's Dyke and has become known in recent years as the Whitford Dyke. Works with this profile of a central bank and shallow ditches to either side have usually been seen as agreed markers between estates.

Finally, another 2km to the north, traces of earthwork alongside the road between Tre-abbot-bach (SJ 106 785) and Trelawnydd (SJ 090 795) were suggested to further extend Offa's Dyke towards the sea, although a 5.75km gap remained between here and Prestatyn (SJ 043 830) where Fox considered the Dyke ended.

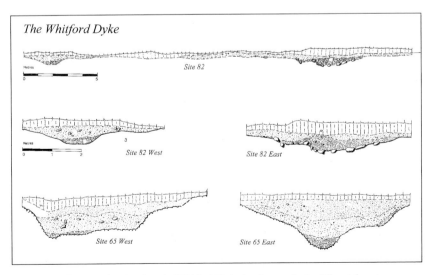

52 *Section drawings showing that the Whitford Dyke is of a completely different form to Offa's Dyke*

A number of excavations have taken place on these two lengths and are detailed below:

Site 121, A55 Improvement, Whitford (SJ 136 759)
The A55 road improvements in 1986 intersected the line suggested by Fox between Pen-y-gelli and Ysceifiog. We considered that the south-eastern end of the Whitford Dyke had been found in Pen-y-gelli wood but took the opportunity to examine the extensive cutting through which the new road was to run some 500m further south. The site was visited on numerous occasions in the course of the year and at various stages of the work, but no evidence of an earthen bank was found nor any trace of a ditch, whether rock-cut ditches similar to those found at site 23 to the north or a ditch cut through the subsoils.

Site 83, Pen-y-gelli, Whitford (SJ 135 764) (**52**)
The surface evidence for the south-eastern end of the Whitford Dyke is to be seen in Pen-y-gelli wood. In 1981 the line of the Whitford Dyke was projected a short way into the wood and a section cut across it. The full length of the trench showed a thin orange-brown loam overlying the limestone bedrock. There was no discernable feature within the trench that suggested ditches had ever been present here and it was concluded that the Whitford Dyke did not continue beyond the surface evidence.

Site 82, Rhydwen Farm, Whitford (SJ 133 766)
The line of the Whitford Dyke crosses arable fields at Rhydwen Farm and we were given permission to open up a 2m-wide trench across the feature for a length of 26m. The plough soil was removed to reveal the remains of a stone bank 12m wide and surviving to a height of only a few centimetres. This had been constructed from the excavation of ditches on either side of the bank, which were only 0.5m deep and 4.5m wide. This was clearly not comparable to Offa's Dyke.

Site 65, Brynbella (1979), Whitford (SJ 129 771)
The ditches were also excavated to either side of a standing hedge 400m to the west of site 82 and similar features were revealed. The hedge stood on the central bank and was flanked by the rock-cut ditches. This excavation was a reopening of Fox's 1925 excavations (our site 1) across the linear earthwork to the north-west of Brynbella mound.

Site 88, Cornel Cae, Whitford (SJ 125 775)

The earthwork present in this woodland further to the north-west of Brynbella is of a different form and character, with fragile banks and a minor ditch, and it is separate from the Whitford Dyke and not a continuation of it.

It is so important a fact for Dyke studies that this earthwork is not a part of Offa's Dyke that the reasoning should be summarised here. Firstly, the earthwork is not physically connected to Offa's Dyke, the south-east termination has been found in Pen-y-gelli wood and the earthwork does not cross the line of the A55; secondly, the gap between the Whitford Dyke and the northern ending of the central portion of Offa's Dyke is 22.75km (14 miles); thirdly, although the reason for attempting to join this work to Offa's Dyke is the belief that Offa's Dyke should run from sea to sea, this Whitford Dyke still stops short of the sea at Prestatyn by 4.83km (3 miles); but fourthly, and most decisive of all, the whole nature and construction of the Whitford Dyke is completely different from any known part of Offa's Dyke, consisting as it does of two ditches, one on either side of a low central bank rather than the Offa's Dyke pattern of a strong bank with a single western ditch.

It should not be the purpose of the present authors to criticise our pioneering predecessors. However, Sir Cyril Fox did believe that he could recognise the 'Western frontier works of Mercia in the seventh and eighth centuries' from surface evidence. The touchstone was that the 'work', whether a hedge, a bank or a road, proceeded in the 'right' direction, that is in the direction Fox thought the Dyke should go to fill a perceived gap. His fieldwork identified various other features north of the Whitford Dyke as being a part of Offa's Dyke and consequently some of these became Scheduled Ancient Monuments. Thus, when road widening threatened such a length, we were asked to excavate in advance of its destruction at:

Site 18, Tre-abbot-bach, Whitford (SJ 112 784)

The hedgebank and the grass verge to its front were carefully excavated and all was demonstrated to be post-medieval, securely dated on ceramic evidence. We moved into the field to the north and mechanically excavated *into the natural* limestone. This work was carried out in 1973, in the early days of the Project, and it was difficult to adjust to the fact that a Scheduled Ancient Monument was in fact an enclosure bank although we had by then three trenches at right angles to the scheduled line. In an attempt to resolve this *impasse* we opened:

Site 17, Village, Trelawnyd (SJ 089 798)

In Trelawnyd the Rural District Council had pulled down some cottages prior to re-development of their site. Fox's line of the Dyke was meant to pass through the gardens of these cottages. We excavated mechanically a 2m-wide trench down to undisturbed natural deposits and found no sign of any identifiable dyke, neither bank nor ditch.

Further investigations were carried out at:

Site 28, Pentre Ffyddion, Trelawnyd (SJ 104 790)

Offa's Dyke Project carried out this excavation in 1976 for the Department of the Environment in advance of deep ploughing. The site was a crop mark that had been scheduled as Offa's Dyke. Traces of a minor track and accompanying hedgebank were found that predated the turnpike road and the reorganisation of the fields. No evidence was found for a bank or ditch that could have represented a defensive Dyke.

Site 192, Water Main, Trelawnyd East (SJ 094 797) Earthworks

A watching brief carried out on the A5151 examined a machine-cut trench for a water main. The trench was only about 0.5m wide and 1m deep, but was 100m long and revealed no evidence of a structure consistent with a Dyke although it was noted that it could have been at a deeper level.

Site 142, Rose and Crown, Trelawnyd (SJ 092 797) CPAT

Two excavations were carried out by Clwyd-Powys Archaeological Trust for Cadw in advance of housing development. The first trench was outside the scheduled area and found that the ground had been much disturbed by large pits filled with post-medieval building rubble. If there had ever been evidence for an earthwork here, it had been destroyed. The second trench was within the scheduled area and showed what appeared to be a considerable artificial build-up of brown silt up to 0.5m deep and 10m wide that could be the remains of a bank. This feature coincided with a ridge visible on the surface of the field. No dating evidence was found, no buried soil was found and no evidence was found for a ditch.

To summarise, there are two short but complete earthworks between Treuddyn and the sea, each of which hinges on a circular feature – the more southerly on Ysceifiog Bronze Age barrow and the more northerly on Brynbella mound. The length at Trelawnyd never existed.

Thus no evidence in the entire length north of Treuddyn can even remotely be identified as Offa's Dyke. This is not a surprising conclusion, for, even if all the suggested line from Treuddyn to Prestatyn had been acceptable; it would follow no known natural frontier, no agricultural or topographical division, and no linguistic or historic border. It is a line invented to fill a perceived gap, and the attempt to close these 'gaps' had led to a great deal of effort that has finally succeeded in disproving the 'sea to sea' theory that has been accepted for so long.

Other earthworks in the Welsh Marches

This book is concerned with Offa's Dyke but we have from time to time referred to Wat's Dyke and other earthworks in the region. In a chronological scheme devised by Cyril Fox and accepted by Frank Stenton, they were woven into a pattern of explanation of the development of the *Western Frontier Works of Mercia*. Fox believed that the earliest linear earthworks were a group of banks and ditches, known collectively since his work as the Short Dykes. The list of the works discussed in his book was supplied to him by the great indexer and fieldworker, Lily (Lal) Chitty and although she prepared lists for other areas along the Marches, Fox used only those from a limited area, mainly in Shropshire and Montgomeryshire. This in itself has led to a misunderstanding by some fieldworkers and interpreters of the Dykes that this group was unique along the border.

The Short Dykes were believed by Fox to date from early in the Anglo-Saxon period and were built to close or control ridgeways and valleys. Our work has shown that they are indeed short earthworks,

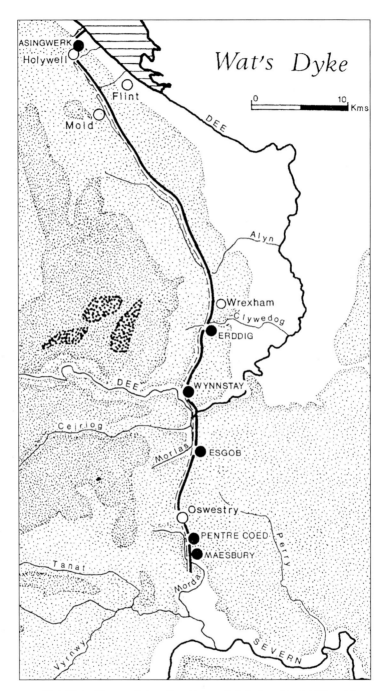

53 *Wat's Dyke. The use of the valley sides, particularly from Esgob Mill, and its position to the east of the higher ground can clearly be seen. The large number of excavations on this earthwork has not been marked but a complete list can be found in appendix 2*

complete in themselves, that either lie across the spine of a ridgeway or across a valley bottom to finish on the rising ground at either side of the valley. They do not join together to make longer earthworks. Very little dating is available for the Short Dykes but our work has shown that the Rowe Ditch in Herefordshire belongs to the Anglo-Saxon period and is earlier than the tenth century; the Whitford Dyke in the north has been shown to be along a medieval boundary and is typical of boundaries of this later date as it has a ditch to both sides of the bank. We also consider that the earthwork across the Beachley peninsula near Chepstow should be placed into the category of Short Dykes. Short linear earthworks from other areas have been dated and can range from early in the prehistoric period to Tudor, and the surface evidence is not always a clear indication of their date. Thus a single date and purpose for this disparate group of Short Dykes cannot be accepted and we must discount them in any interpretation of Offa's Dyke.

In the chronology of Fox and Stenton, the Short Dykes formed the first stage in the defence of the western frontier of Mercia and the second stage was the building of Wat's Dyke. Offa's Dyke Project has excavated over 60 sites on Wat's Dyke and has surveyed most of its length, and has extended its length southwards for several kilometres.

Wat's Dyke is a shorter earthwork than Offa's Dyke and was built between Lower Morton (SJ 305 233) close to the confluence of the River Morda with the River Vyrnwy in the south to the Dee Estuary at Basingwerk (SJ 195 775) in the north (**53**). Prior to our work it was believed to be 20.75 miles in length, but can now be shown to be 38.6 miles long, a spectacular achievement of fieldwork and excavation. Unfortunately, no secure series of scientific dates has yet been established although a wide range of dates has been suggested by various people. However, we must emphasise that Offa's Dyke and Wat's Dyke run almost parallel to each other in the northern Marches, they both face towards the west, and our excavations have shown that both have many constructional features in common. From these observations it would seem likely that they are roughly contemporary; perhaps within a century or two of each other. However the question of which of these two great earthworks is the earlier must remain open.

APPENDIX 1

RESEARCH STRATEGIES OF OFFA'S DYKE PROJECT

The research by the group now known as Offa's Dyke Project was begun in the early 1970s by David Hill with Manchester Extra-Mural Students who wanted to do fieldwork rather than listen to lectures. A strong interest, indeed a passionate interest, to understand Anglo-Saxon England, led them to the only major monuments of the period in easy reach of Manchester – Offa's Dyke and Wat's Dyke. Armed with a knowledge of what Cyril Fox had written, the decision was taken to investigate the places where Fox said that no earthwork had ever been built. He explained these gaps by either an 'impassable ravine' or by 'impenetrable forest'. The latter was an offshoot of the very popular theory in academic circles of the 1920s and 1930s that held that one could reconstitute dense woodlands on the heavy clay for the early medieval period. This would lead to the cold, wet woodland, 'jungle', that was impenetrable to roving warbands. However, this concept of the nature of eighth-century woodland was misconceived. The woods were a primary source for fuel, building materials, food for swine and hunting grounds that meant that the woods were open canopy forest, high trees with little underbrush as this was grazed by the animals and managed by man. By the 1970s, the belief in 'impenetrable forest' was no longer held and new techniques for investigation such as air photographs and geophysics were available. The first Martin-Clark resistivity meter may have been a cumbersome tool with five probes and yards of wires that constantly twisted themselves together, but it did produce results. The plot of the line of Wat's Dyke across Bryn-y-Bal Hill and the subsequent excavation of the ditch was our first proof that this could be a fruitful research tool.

Thus the 'Certificate in Methods in Archaeology' was born: a three-year part-time course for adults that concentrated on practical archaeology and which used the Dykes in the Welsh Marches as its training ground. Initially the research aims were to fill in the gaps and to identify the structure of the earthworks. Soon evidence had been gathered together from excavation, from fieldwork, from air photographs and from early maps and documents. It began to be clear that some of the gaps had indeed had the earthwork firmly in place in the past but that farming and urban developments had destroyed the above ground evidence. However the original ditch, 2m deep and at least 7m wide, was still there to be found below ground no matter how unpromising the surface evidence might be.

In those limited areas where very clearly defined questions might be solved, a variety of techniques were applied. Specific problems could be addressed such as 'Was the Dyke ever built here?' 'Were there gateways?' as suggested by Fox and by Noble; 'Was Offa's Dyke built from 'sea to sea' and if so where was it in the north and the south?' One technique, which always seems to promise a great deal, is aerial photography. The viewing of a site from above, either as a shadow thrown by a low sun over a denuded earthwork or, where a site is completely erased at the surface, by parch marks or differences in growth or ripening of a crop. Obtaining aerial photographs can be a costly and time-consuming activity and it was only on rare occasions that we were able to fly in a light aircraft or helicopter to take photographs, but we were fortunate to be working at the same time as Chris Musson, then with Clwyd-Powys Archaeological Trust based in Welshpool, and his frequent flights along the Welsh Marches and superb photography provided us with a wealth of evidence. We were also able to take our own photographs using a 30ft monopod with a camera attached or a large kite with a radio-activated camera hanging from its base. Both these devices caused much excitement amongst students, one or two near mishaps and very occasionally a really good high-level photograph.

Prospecting at ground level was principally done with a resistivity meter, and early surveys were laborious and the results had to be hand-logged and plotted. Our modern machines, developed by one of our research team, are increasingly sophisticated, easy to use and provide us with some excellent results. We also use the fluxgate gradiometer from time to time but results from this have proved to be less reliable on our particular sites. The basic principle of both machines is to locate the disturbed, and often moister, soil of the fill of the ditch below ground.

Prospecting may give a good indication of potential evidence for Offa's Dyke, but ultimately excavation is needed to show that the anomalies plotted do indeed represent the ditch, for the ditch is our diagnostic feature. Remains of the bank can be of any height or width and usually contain no dating material or evidence of structure, but the original ditch of Offa's Dyke was almost always dug to a depth of 2m (6ft) and a width of 7m (28ft). This is, of course, far larger than any normal field boundary ditch. On excavation, the layers of silt and infill show clearly as different in colour and texture from the undisturbed soils into which the ditch was cut. These fills may also contain artefacts such as pottery or metalwork that could help to show the manmade nature of the feature or to at least suggest the time when the ditch was infilled. Ecofacts found in the ditch fills such as snail shells or pollen grains can also tell us something of the vegetational history of the area round the ditch throughout the time it was open or filling in. When the excavation is complete and all the fills of the ditch have been removed, the original profile of the ditch can be observed and drawn for future reference.

Gradually an increasingly large body of evidence accumulated and a group of students and former students were well trained to continue the research. The increasing awareness that upstanding lengths of Offa's Dyke were gradually being destroyed by natural processes and by the work of man brought about the decision to record the earthwork in more detail – a methodology for this survey was evolved and the group became Offa's Dyke Project under the joint direction of the present authors. The survey was intended to be complete in itself but was also to serve as a tool for a better understanding of the Dyke and to point the way to places where a modest-sized excavation could add to our existing knowledge. Thus sites where the questions of gateways and water-crossing places might be profitably investigated more intensively could be identified. This system of recording is given in detail below because, although the result will not be found in this book, it has contributed greatly to our understanding of the monument and this understanding is discussed in the preceeding chapters.

The survey methodology was initially based on that devised for the Research Committee of the Society of Antiquaries of London and reported in the *Antiquaries Journal* in 1946. This was to a very large extent based on the work of Cyril Fox on Offa's Dyke, and brought with it his beliefs and prejudices, and we quickly developed what we believe to be a more objective and thorough system of recording. The aim was that this should be both an accurate record and an objective one. It also needed to be one that did not require complex equipment or large sums of money as neither were available. The decision to survey Offa's Dyke was almost as daunting as it must have been when Offa first informed the *witan* and the shire-reeves that he intended building it. Even taking the central portion of 64 miles of earthwork, it was best not to consider how long it would take in case we never began. Therefore, partly for ease of reference and partly so that a feeling of progress would be achieved, the whole length of Offa's Dyke, as defined by Fox, was divided up into 5km lengths as measured due north on the Ordnance Survey grid. Wat's Dyke was treated in the same way and so we now had a research project based on 39 fascicules, each 5km long, on Offa's Dyke and 12 on Wat's Dyke. In addition to these major earthworks, the earthworks described by Fox as Short Dykes were also to be included in the investigation.

The fieldwork is based on the 1:2500 Ordnance Survey sheets and, as both Offa's Dyke and Wat's Dyke run almost due north/south for most of their length, the system of giving eastings and northings when referring to survey points was abandoned in favour of northings only. This means that the two-letter Ordnance Survey grid square reference can be followed by a five figure northing rather than a full ten figure one. This system is found to be less confusing during fieldwork and easier when filing the results. The maps are also used to record information about where the lengths of the earthwork that are Scheduled Ancient Monuments are located, who the landowners and tenants are and to locate the surveyed profile points and the excavations. Accompanying the maps are the survey results, a written description of how the monument sits in the landscape and the state of the monument at the time of the survey. Information from early maps, from Fox, and other fieldwork and descriptions are also noted.

The measured survey is related to Ordnance Datum throughout and so the first task is to establish temporary benchmarks along the stretch to be surveyed, ensuring that they are accurate by checking between two Ordnance Survey benchmarks. Accuracy here is usually to within a centimetre, the longest run to date between benchmarks being 7km. The two main elements of the survey, the profiles and the longitudinal section, are then carried out simultaneously, but are here described individually for clarity (**54**).

The profiles are recorded at 100m intervals as measured along the length of the earthwork regardless of its state of preservation at that point. If, however, the ground has been so altered as to render such a profile meaningless, as for example where a railway or major road now crosses the line, then only a single spot height is taken. The profile line is laid out at right angles to the perceived line of the crest of the bank and readings are taken, using a dumpy level, at metre intervals for 18m to each side of the centre point on the bank. The aim is to give a representative sample of the present state of the earthwork. When drawn, all surveyed heights above sea level are included to enable a redrawing to take place should it be considered necessary. Hedge and fence lines are accurately measured and marked on the profile (**55**).

The second element of the survey, the longitudinal section, is measured at 25m intervals along the line of the earthwork. At each point three readings are taken, one at the top of the bank, one at the bottom of the ditch and one on the outer lip of the ditch. Where no

54 *Students surveying Offa's Dyke on Rushock Hill, looking east with Box Folly on the horizon and Herefordshire Plain in the mists beyond*

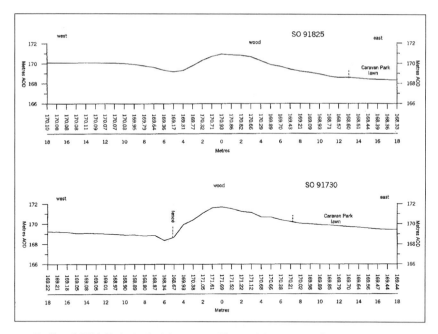

55 *Profiles of Offa's Dyke in the Montgomery Plain at SO 257 917 and SO 257 918. Working drawings by Sheila Rawson for Offa's Dyke Project*

monument is visible, a reading is taken on the perceived line of the crest of the bank and at 5m and 10m to its west to show the slope of the ground. These readings are used to draw three lines that represent the ground level, the bottom of the ditch and the top of the bank. As the readings are taken to Ordnance Datum, the trace along the earthwork shows where it is on rising ground and where it is on falling ground. The top of the bank and the bottom of the ditch are plotted at right angles to the line representing the ground. Various scales have to be used in the plot to give a meaningful impression of the situation on the ground. The linear length is plotted at 1:2500 to fit with the scale of the maps and allow direct comparisons to be made with them. The vertical scale for the ground level is 1:400 as this shows the rise and fall of the land without too much exaggeration. The vertical scale for the bank and for the ditch plots is at 1:200 which allows an impression of the height of the bank and depth of the ditch in relation to the ground level to be formed, again without too much exaggeration. Any gaps are measured and plotted together with rivers, roads and field boundaries. As with the profiles, the actual heights above Ordnance Datum are given at the bottom edge of the drawing (**56**).

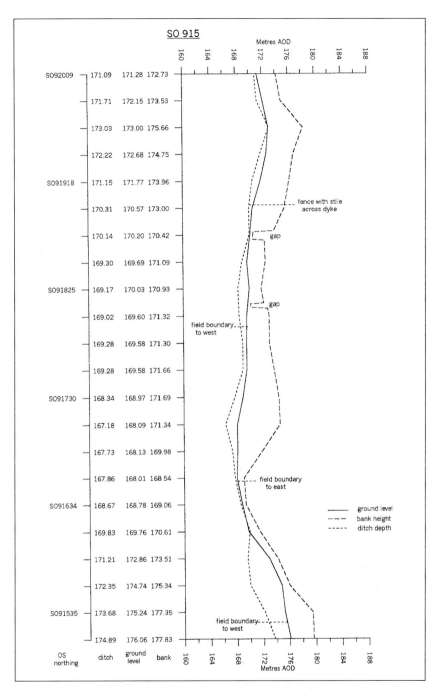

56 *Longitudinal section of Offa's Dyke in the Montgomery Plain from SO 256 915. The height of the bank and depth of the ditch are exaggerated in relation to ground level, actual heights above Ordnance Datum are given on axes. Working drawing by Sheila Rawson for Offa's Dyke Project*

The written description is made during the survey and after the readings have been drawn up the length is walked again checking that all the details appear to be correct. In recent years the demise of the Extra-Mural Department at Manchester has reduced the amount of work it has been possible to complete. The research is now directed from Porth y waen Study Centre and a small group of the experienced students, some of whom have now worked on the monuments for 20 years, have continued with the field survey, mainly in the winter months when the leaves are off the trees, and excavations have taken place each summer to try to answer outstanding questions.

One of the most important aspects to emerge from all of this work has been the opportunity to spend long hours walking up and down the same stretch, first on the bank side then on the ditch side, from south to north and from north to south. It is surprising how different it can appear as the line of approach varies. In writing the descriptions the author (Margaret Worthington) has also had to think carefully about how the earthwork is situated in the landscape; why here and not on the higher hill or why does it curve here and run straight there. A major Dyke system is complex and it can be difficult to present a clear picture of its character and what might have been in the minds of the men who first laid it out. It is, however, essential that such a picture be gained, as it is this that allows us to go on to suggest a purpose for so massive an expenditure of time and energy in the original building of the Dyke.

The survey is far from complete – it will probably never be completed – but important insights have been gained from those sections that have been examined in such great detail. It is now possible to appreciate the very careful siting of the line in the landscape. It is extremely sensitive to the nuances of the topography as it curves round a minor knoll to keep the advantage of both the slope and the view to the west. These observations are now brought to each length walked and increasingly the unity of thought behind its build is recognised.

APPENDIX 2
SOURCES

Source 1
The Ordinance concerning the *Dunsæte*

The translation below comes from a duplicated sheet given to one of the authors (David Hill) many years ago by Frank Noble and is signed F.N. 7.2.69.

The manuscript is Cambridge, Corpus Christi College 383, which is Ker No. 65 article 23. It is dated to the middle of the eleventh to twelfth century and is probably from St Paul's, London. It is a collection of laws, though no explanation exists for why this particular law code appears at this point in the collection. Sir Frank Stenton, in *Anglo-Saxon England*, discusses the meeting of King Athelstan with the five Welsh kings at Hereford when they submitted to Athelstan's over-lordship and agreed to pay substantial tribute in AD 927. Stenton goes on to suggest that it was at this time that the boundary between the English and the Welsh along the River Wye near Hereford could have been agreed, although the extant document is a later copy.

Ðis seo gerædnes ðe Angelcynnes witan 7 Wealhðeode rædboran betweox Dunsetan gestetton

This is the agreement which the English Witan and the councillors of the Welsh people have established among the *Dunsæte*:

Ðæt is gif man trode bedrifð for stolenes yrfes of stæde on oðer, ðonne befæste man flaet spo[r] landesmannum oððe mid mearce gecyfle, flæt man rhit drife.

That is, if anyone follows the track of stolen cattle from one riverbank to the other, then he must hand over the tracking to the men of the land, or show by some mark that the track is rightfully pursued.

Fo se syððan to ðe flæt land age 7 hæbbe him ða æscan; 7 ðæs on IX nihton gylde flæt yrfe oððe to ðam dæge underwed lecge, flæt sy ðæs orfes oðeer healf weorð, 7 ðæs on IX nihton flæt wed unde mid rihtan gylde.

The man who owns that land must take up the search himself and within nine days he must compensate for the cattle, or deposit on that day a pledge worth half as much again as the cattle. Within nine days from then he must redeem that pledge with the right compensation.

Gif man secge, flæt trod awaoh drife, ðonne mot se ðe flæt yrfe ah trod [o]ð to stæðe lædan 7 ðær syxn sum ungecorenra, ðe getrywe syn, ðone aðsyllan, flæt he mid folcrhite on flæt land sprece, swa his [orf]ðær up eode.

If it is said that the track is being wrongfully followed then the man that owns the cattle must trace the track to the bank, and there six (unselected) men of good repute, himself being one, must swear that he claims with folk-right against that land because his cattle went across there.

Æfre ymb IX niht gebyreð betweox ðam stæðum, flæt man oðrum riht wyrce ge æt lade ge ætælcere spræce, fle him betweox bið.

Always, after nine days, right ought to be done by one to another between the (dwellers on) the two banks, both in clearing oneself of charges or of any other dispute between them.

Ne sent nan oðer lad æt tihtlan bute ordal betweox Wealan 7 Ænglan, bute man ðafian wille.

There is no other way, between Welsh and English, of clearing oneself of a charge, except by ordeal, unless his opponent will allow it.

Of ægðran stæðe on oðer man mot badian, bute man elles riht begyton mæge.

A pledge can be seized from the other bank if justice cannot be obtained in any other way.

Gif bad genumen sy on mannes orfe for oðres mannes ðingum, ðonne begyte ða bade ham se, ðe heo fore genumen sy, oððe of his agenum ðone gehalde, ðe flæt orf age:

If a pledge from one man's cattle is seized on another man's account, let the one on whose account it was taken get the pledge back, or let him satisfy from his own possessions the man whose cattle have been taken.

Sceal syððan need riht wyrcean se ðe ær nolde.

Then he will have to do right who would not do it before.

XII lahmen scylon riht becean Wealan 7 Ænglan: VI Englisc 7 VI Wylisce.

Twelve lawmen shall declare what is just to Welsh and English: six of them English, six Welsh.

Ðolien ealles ðæs hy agon, gyf hi who tæcan; oððe gelandian hi, flæt hi het ne cuðon.

Let them forfeit all they possess if they give a wrong judgement, unless they clear themselves as knowing no better.

Ðeah æt stæltyhtlan lad teorie Ængliscan oððe Wiliscan, gylde angyldes flæt he mid beled wæs: ðæs oðres gyldes nan ðing ne ðæs wites ðe ma.

If an Englishman or a Welshman fail to clear himself of a charge of theft, let him pay the simple compensation laid upon him, and no other payment or penalty.

Gyf Wealh Ænglisne man ofslea, ne ðearf he hine hide[r] ofer buton be healfan were gyldan, ne Ænglisc Wylisne geon ofer ðe ma, sy he ðegenboren, sy he ceorlboren: healf wer ðær ætfeald.

If a Welshman kills an Englishman, he need not pay over to his side more than half the man-price; no more than an Englishman for a Welshman to the other side, whether he be thane-born or churl-born; half the wergild falls away.

Nah naðer to farenne ne Wilisc man on Ænglisc land ne Ænglisc on Wylisc ðe ma, butan gesettan landmen, se hine sceal æt stæfle underfon 7 eft ðær butan facne gebringan.

Neither is a Welshman to cross over into English land, nor an Englishman to Welsh without the appointed man from that land, who shall meet him at the bank and bring him back there again without any offence.

Gyf se landman æniges facnes gewita sy, ðonne sy he wites scyldig, buton he hine ðære gewitnesse geladie.

If the man of that land connive at any crime, he shall be liable to the penalty unless he can clear himself of having witnessed it.

Swa eac ælc ðe gewita oððe gewyrhta sy, ðær utlendisc man inlenddiscan derie, geladie ðære midwiste be ðes orfes weorðe; 7 flæt sy cyreað; 7 se ðe hyne belecge, ofga his spræce mid foraðe.

So also, everyone who knows or is involved when a foreigner does harm to a native must clear himself of being an accessory according to the value of the property: that must be done by a select oath, and the accuser must begin his suit with a preliminary oath.

Gif ðeos lad teorie twygylde 7 hlaforde hs wite.

If this defence fails he must pay a double fine and the penalty to the lord.

Hors man sceal gyldan mid XXX scill. oððe be ðam Indian; myran mid XX scill. oððe be ðam, 7 wintersteal ealswa; wilde weorf mid XII scill. oððe be ðam, oxan mid XXX p. cu mid XXIIII p. swyn mid VIII p. man mid punde, sceap mid scill., gat mid II p.

30 shillings shall be paid for a horse, or exculpated at that rate; 20 shillings for a mare, or at that rate; and a 'winter steal' (one-year-old stallion) the same; 'wild weorf' (wild cattle?) 12 shillings, or at that rate; an ox with 30 pence; a cow with 24 pence; a pig with 8 pence; a man with a pound; a sheep with a shilling; a goat with 2 pence.

Oðre ungesawene ðing man mot mid aðe gewyrán, 7 syððan be ðam gyldan.

Other things not seen may be valued on oath and paid for accordingly.

Gif man orf befe, 7 man ofer streame hit tyman sylle, ðonne sette man inhorh oððe undeerwed lecge, flæt seo prec ende hæbbe.

If anything is seized and the possessor wishes to vouch as warrantor someone over the river, let him give security or a pledge so that the case can be concluded.

Se ðe hit him to teo, sylle sixa sum ðone að, flæt he hit him swa to teo swa hit him ðeofstolen wære.

Let anyone who claims it make an oath, himself one of six, that he claims it because it was stolen from him.

7 se ðe hit tyme, sylle ana ðone að, flæt he hit to ðære handa tyme, fle him sealed.

And let the one who claims the right to it give his oath alone, saying he claims it by the warranty of the man who sold it to him.

Gif hit man begeondan str[e]ame agnian wylle, ðone sceal flæt beon mid ordale.

And if anyone from beyond the river wants to make a claim, that must be by ordeal.

Gelice ðam Ænglisc sceal Wliscan riht wyrcean.

In the same way English shall do justice to Welsh.

Hwilan Wentsæte hyrdan into Dunsætan; ac hit gebyreð rihtor into Westsexan: ðyder hy scylan gafol 7 gislas syllan.

Formerly the *Wentsæte* (people of Gwent) belonged to the *Dunsæte*, but more correctly they belong to the West Saxons: and they have to send tribute and hostages there.

Eac Dunsæte beflyrfan, gif heom se cyning an, flæt man huru friðgislas to heom læte.

But the *Dunsæte* also need, if the king will grant it to them, that at least they should be allowed hostages for peace.

The Pillar of Eliseg
Source 2

The original inscription of 31 lines was recorded by the Antiquary Edward Llwyd in 1696 and a facsimile copy is extant. This copy was quoted in full by Nash-Williams in the *Inscribed Stones of Wales* (No. 182) and is quoted here.

+ CONCENN FILIUS CATTELL CATELL
+Concenn son of Cattell, Cattell

FILIUS BROHCMAIL BRAHCMA(i)L FILIUS
son of Brohcmail, Brohcmail son

ELISEG ELISEG FILIUS GUOILLAUC
of Eliseg, Eliseg son of Guoillauc

+CONCENN ITAQUE PRONEPOS ELISEG
+Concenn therefore being great-grandson of Eliseg

EDIFICAUIT HUNC LAPIDEM PRO AUO
erected this stone to his great-grandfather

SUO ELISEG
Eliseg

+IPSE EST ELISEG QUI NEC(?)
+It is Eliseg who annexed

XIT HEREDITATEM POUO(i)S [—
the inheritance of Powys . . .

—] PER VIIII [ANNOS (?)] E POTESTATE ANGLO
throughout nine (years?) from the power of the English

RUM IN GLADIO SUO PARTA IN IGNE
which he made into a sword-land by fire

[+QUIC]UMQUE RECIT[A]UERIT MANESCRIP
+Whosoever shall read this hand-inscribed

[TUM LAPID]EM DET BENEDICTIONEM SUPE
stone, let him give a blessing on

[R ANIMA]M ELISEG +IPSE EST CONCENN
the soul of Eliseg. +It is Concenn

[—] MANU
who . . . with his hand

[-] AD REGNUM SUUM POUO(i)S
. . . to his own kingdom of Powys

[-] ET QUOD
. . . and which

[-]

...

[-] MONTEM
... the mountain

(one line wanting, possibly more)

[-] MONARCHIAM
... the monarchy

[-] MAXIMUS BRITTANIAE
Maximus ... of Britain ...

[CONCE]NN PASCEN[T] MAUN ANNAN
Concenn, Pascent, ... Maun, Annan.

[+] BRITU A[U]T[E]M FILIUS GUARTHI
+Britu, moreover, (was) the son of Guorthigirn (i.e. Vortigern),

[GIRN] QUE(m) BENED[IXIT] ROMANO
whom Germanus blessed and

[QU]E PEPERIT EI SE[V]IRA FILIA MAXIMI
whom Severa bore to him, the daughter of Maximus
R[EG]IS QUI OCCIDIT REGEM ROMANO
the king, who slew the king of the Romans.

RUN + CONMARCH PINXIT HOC
+Conmarch painted this

CHIROGRAF(i)U(m) REGE SUO POSCENTE
writing at the command of his king

CONCENN + BENEDICTIO D(omi)NI IN CON
Concenn. +The blessing of the Lord (be) upon Concenn

CENN ET S(uo)S I(n) TOTA FAMILIA EIUS
and all members of his family

ET IN TOTA(m) [RE]GIONE(m) POUOIS
and upon all the land of Powys

USQUE IN [DIEM IUDICII AMEN (?)].
until the Day of Judgement. Amen.

APPENDIX 3
GAZETTEER OF SITES

Offa's Dyke		*Site*
SO 270 639	Newcastle, Newcastle Hill	62
SO 285 721	Knighton, Frydd Road [CPAT, 1976]	48
SO 284 726	Knighton, Pinner's Hole	16
SO 284 735	Llanfair Waterdine, Kinsley Wood	80
SO 254 808	Clun, Spoad Hill [SCC, 1992]	168
SO 263 887	Mainstone, River Unk	98
SO 259 893	Edenhope, Nutwood	128
SO 258 896	Castlewright, Kerry Ridgeway	56
SO 258 896	Castlewright, Agger [Houghton, 1957-60]	20
SO 251 933	Brompton and Rhiston, The Blue Bell [SCC Highways, 1984]	111
SO 251 933	Brompton Hall, Paddock	133
SO 243 954	Brompton and Rhiston, Lower Gwarthlow	157
SO 237 967	Chirbury, Dudston Covert	156
SO 236 972	Chirbury, Chirbury South	155
SO 235 972	Chirbury, Chirbury North	154
SO 236 974	Chirbury, Barker's Fort	110
SO 235 974	Chirbury, Chirbury Road	153
SO 234 979	Chirbury, Rownal Covert	55
SO 233 979	Chirbury, Rownal Covert	152
SO 233 980	Chirbury, Calves Ground	151
SO 232 984	Chirbury, Rownal Paddock	150
SO 232 992	Chirbury, River Camlad	117
SO 232 993	Forden, River Camlad	118
SJ 240 022	Forden [CPAT, 1987]	143
SJ 243 028	Forden, Bryn Hafod (1976)	27
SJ 234 028	Forden, Bryn Hafod [Fox, 1929]	6

The Herefordshire Plain

Rowe Ditch

Grimsditch

Lyonshall

The Wye Valley to the sea

The North from Treuddyn to the Coast

Wat's Dyke

SJ 334 523	Acton, Wat's Dyke School	12
SJ 312 569	Hope, Rhydyn Hall	53
SJ 309 587	Hope, Pen-y-Bryn [CPAT, 1997/8]	202
SJ 309 587	Hope [CPAT, 1989]	164
SJ 306 593	Hope, Pigeon House Farm	15
SJ 299 607	Hope, Clawdd Offa	58
SJ 264 636	Mold Rural, Bod Offa Farm	76
SJ 263 637	Mold Rural, Watergate Estate	75
SJ 261 638	Mynydd Isa Garden Centre [Earthworks, 1998]	189
SJ 262 638	Mynydd Isa Water Main [Earthworks, 1996]	190
SJ 262 639	Mynydd Isa, Varley's Trench [Varley, 1957]	34
SJ 257 649	Bryn-y-baal [CPAT, 1991]	195
SJ 257 653	Mold, Bypass	14
SJ 254 656	Soughton, Sewage Treatment Works [CPAT, 1993]	197
SJ 252 659	Soughton, Ditch	11
SJ 252 659	Soughton, Pipeline	25
SJ 247 663	Soughton, Entrance [CPAT 1995]	199
SJ 248 663	Soughton, Tenant Farm [Earthworks 1997]	188
SJ 243 670	Soughton, Clawdd Offa	13
SJ 233 691	Northop, Middle Mill [CPAT, 1984]	103
SJ 233 691	Northop, Middle Mill [Fraser & Bevan Evans, 1955]	10
SJ 232 698	Northop, Coed Llys [CPAT, 1986]	132
SJ 232 698	Flint Mountain, Coed Llys	131
SJ 232 698	Flint Mountain, Bryn-y-Garreg	35
SJ 216 726	Flint, Fernside Cottage	39
SJ 216 726	Flint, Nant y Fflint Pipeline [Earthworks, 1995]	169
SJ 214 730	Flint, Glyn Cottage	136
SJ 213 731	Flint, Bethel Chapel	38
SJ 205 737	Bagillt, Cefn Farm (S)	159
SJ 205 737	Bagillt, Cefn Farm (N)	160
SJ 199 742	Bagillt, Cefn Lane	138
SJ 198 745	Holywell, Coetia Clwyd	36
SJ 196 747	Holywell, Coed llywybr-y-bi	37
SJ 191 767	Coed Strand, Cupid's Grove	57

BIBLIOGRAPHY

MAPS

Evans, John, 1795, *Map of the Six Counties of North Wales*, Llwyngroes.

Speed, John, 1676, *The Theatre of the Empire of Great Britain, Part 2 Wales*, London

Williams, William, 1720, *A New Map of the Counties of Denbigh and Flint*, Oswestry.

ORIGINAL SOURCES

Anglo-Saxon Chronicle: Swanton, Michael, translator and editor, 1996, *The Anglo-Saxon Chronicle*, Dent, London

Annales Cambriae: see Nennius

Asser: conveniently, Keynes, S. and Lapidge, M., 1983, *Alfred the Great: Asser's Life of King Alfred and other contemporary sources*, Penguin Books, Harmondsworth

Bede: conveniently, Leo Sherley-Price, trans (revised R.E Latham) 1968, *A History of the English Church and People*, Penguin, Harmonsworth.

Fox, Cyril, Fieldwork Notebooks in National Museum of Wales archives, Cardiff.

Gildas: Winterbotton, Michael, ed. & trans., 1978, *Gildas: The Ruin of Britain and other documents*, Phillimore, Chichester.

Llandaff Charters: Davies, Wendy, 1978, *An early Welsh microcosm, studies in the Llandaff Charters*, Royal Historical Society, London. Also: Davies, Wendy, 1979, *The Llandaff Charters*, National Library of Wales, Aberystwyth.

Nennius: Morris, John, ed., 1980: *British History and the Welsh Annals*, Phillimore, Chichester.

Pennant: John Rhys, ed., 1883, *Thomas Pennant Tours in Wales*, Caernarvon.

Royal Frankish Annals: *Annales Regni Francorum*, trans B. Scholz, 1970, Ann Arbor.

William of Malmesbury: Mynors R.A.B., Thomson, R.A., Winterbotton M. eds., 1998, *Gesta Regnum Anglorum,* Oxford Medieval Texts, Oxford.

SECONDARY SOURCES

Davies, Wendy, 1982, *Wales in the Early Middle Ages*, Leicester University Press, London.

Earle, J., 1857,'Offa's Dyke, in the neighbourhood of Knighton', *Archaeologia. Cambrensis.*, 3rd series, No.10, 196-209.

Fox, Sir Cyril, 1955, *Offa's Dyke. A field survey of the western frontier-works of Mercia in the seventh and eight centuries.* With a foreword by Sir Frank Stenton., Oxford University Press for British Academy, London.

Fox, Sir Cyril et al., 1946, 'Linear Earthworks: Methods of Field Survey. Notes prepared at the request of the research committee', *Antiquaries Journal*, XXV, 175-9

Gelling, Margaret, ed. 1983, *Offa's Dyke Reviewed* British Archaeological Report 114, Oxford. Carries the subtitle: *Offa's Dyke through the diocese of Hereford, with a critical re-assessment of published work and accepted opinions by Frank Noble (prepared for publication by Margaret Gelling). Being chapters 4 and 5 of a thesis submitted in 1977 for a degree of Master of Philosophy of the Open University.*

Gelling, Margaret, 1978, *Signposts to the Past*, Dent, London.

Hill, David, 1969, 'Burghal Hidage: the establishment of a text', *Medieval Archaeology*, XIII, 84-92.

Houghton, A. W. J., 1957-70, 'The Roman Road from Greenforge through the Central Marches', *Transactions of Shropshire Archaeological Society*, LVI, 233-243.

Hoyle, Jon & Vallender Jo., 1996 (draft), *Offa's Dyke in Gloucestershire: A Management Survey,* Planning Department, Gloucester CC,

Lewis, J. R., 1963, 'A section of Offa's Dyke at Buttington Tump, Tidenham', *Transactions of Bristol and Gloucestershire Archaeological Society*, 92, 202-4.
Lewis, S., 1833, *Topographical Dictionary of Wales* (2 Volumes), S. Lewis & Co., London.

Llwyd, Edward, 1703, *Parochialia*, (*Archaeologia Cambrensis* Supplement, 1911, iii, 96).

McKenny Hughes, T., 1893, 'On Offa's Dyke', *Archaeologia*, liii, 465-484.

Noble, Frank, 1978, *Offa's Dyke re-viewed, a critical re-assessment of published work and accepted opinions; with detailed reconsideration of the course of the Dyke through the Diocese of Hereford*, M.Phil. Thesis for The Open University. See also Gelling M

Rennell, Frances J. R. R., 2nd Baron, 1958, *Valley on the March, a history of a group of manors on the Herefordshire March of Wales*, London.

Royal Commission Inventor, Flintshire, 1912.

Stenton, Sir F. M., 1955, introduction to Cyril Fox 'Offa's Dyke'.

Victoria County History of Shropshire

Wheeler, R.E.M., 1923, Report, *Bulletin of Board of Celtic Studies* Vol 1

INDEX

References in **bold** denote page numbers of illustrations